The Way of the Warrior
Stories of the Crow People

Compiled and Translated by Henry Old Coyote
and Barney Old Coyote Jr.

Edited by Phenocia Bauerle

University of Nebraska Press
Lincoln and London

First Nebraska paperback printing: 2004

Library of Congress
Cataloging-in-Publication Data
Old Coyote, Henry.
The way of the warrior:
stories of the Crow people /
compiled and translated by
Henry Old Coyote and
Barney Old Coyote, Jr.;
edited by Phenocia Bauerle.
p.   cm.
Includes index.
ISBN 0-8032-3572-0 (cloth: alk. paper)
1. Crow Indians—History.
2. Crow Indians—Biography.
3. Oral tradition—Montana.
I. Old Coyote, Barney.
II. Bauerle, Phenocia.   III. Title.
E99.C92 O52   2003
978.6004'9752—dc21
2002032257

ISBN 0-8032-6230-2 (paper: alk. paper)

This book is dedicated to the memory of
Henry Drew Old Coyote Chiilap Baa Alaxileetash (Brave Bull).

It was his vision, foresight, and love for his people and the Crow way
of life that made this work possible. His lifelong goal was to perpetuate that
way of life. He continues to be an inspiration and role model
to his loved ones, the Crow people.

Contents

Illustrations

Preface

It was during the summer of 2000 that I first read the Crow narratives "Rabbit Child: A Crazy Dog of the Crows," "The Saga of Red Bear," "Elusive Fame and Glory: The Story of Spotted Horse," and "The Years Following the Red Lodge," transcribed by the brothers Henry and Barney Old Coyote. I was directing an advanced level undergraduate research project with Phenocia Bauerle, and she asked if she could include the work done by her grandfathers Barney and his brother Henry. (In the Crow tradition, uncles also are regarded as fathers, and great uncles as grandfathers, and so on.) I should mention that my attachment to the Old Coyote family goes back nearly thirty years. When I came to Montana State University in Bozeman in September 1973 I met Barney Old Coyote Jr., who had been hired as the first professor of Indian Studies in July 1970. He had created and was the director of the fledgling Native American Studies program while also teaching Crow in the Modern Languages Department. We became compatriots, as each of us was to bring diversity to both the campus faculty and academic disciplines. Yet when we knew each other then, I had no idea that Barney Old Coyote Jr. was a distinguished World War II veteran, or that Henry and Barney had already transcribed the stories you will be reading in this volume. Phenocia's mother, Patricia Bauerle, is also a treasured friend of many years. While Pat is primarily known in Bozeman as a gifted junior high school teacher, I would be remiss if I did not mention that when she was president of the Indian Club at Montana State University during the mid-1970s, she organized the first Native American Awareness Week, which culminated in an annual Montana State University Pow-Wow, an event that has continued to enrich our university life and the entire Bozeman community for twenty-five years. Her daughter, Phenocia Bauerle, the editor of this collection, is my academic advisee, an outstanding student, and a treasured friend. Thus, I came to the material you will be reading as one who loves and admires the Old Coyote family.

That said, imagine my amazement as I read the following Crow narratives for the first time, oral stories that tribal members had told and retold since the mid-1800s, one over fifty pages in length when transcribed. The stories encompass the falls from grace as well as the military prowess that delineate the behaviors appropriate to Crow leadership and honor. They also are so rich in detail that we can shape a much more informed vision of life in the northwest Rockies of the nineteenth century for Native peoples before the massive influx of European and Asian migrants changed their lives forever. Note that although our American mythology presents Lewis and Clark as the "discoverers" of this vast new territory, goods from the fur trades were already in exchange and commerce quickened dramatically after 1805. These stories mention not only horses (which arrived with the Spanish), but guns, Hudson Bay blankets, handheld telescopes, and trading posts. The narratives are precious because there are so few historical and legendary accounts from the period in which white contact had been made but the traditional lives of indigenous peoples had not been radically altered. New products, new forms of warfare or of travel had been incorporated into their cultural dynamics. Nonetheless, traditional ways had not yet been suppressed.

It is not only the subject matter that amazed me on that first reading, it is the excellence of Henry's and Barney's translations. Their ear for the transcription of orality into written English, the sense of the dramatic, engaged storyteller that pervades each narrative, is what enabled me to suggest to Phenocia that she consider editing their work via our Independent Research 470 class throughout the following academic year.

And here I must speak of Phenocia's and my process and how impressed I have been by the spirit, heart, and mind Phenocia has brought to the work. My editorial concerns focused on grammatical and spelling consistency, paragraph formatting, and questions that a non-Crow might have. I wrote corrections on the manuscript copy, asked questions in the margins, outlined some paragraph units, and made a few suggestions for reordering to make the narrative flow easier for the reader. From the start, I informed Phenocia that she and Barney Old Coyote Jr. were the arbiters of all my suggestions or corrections. Phenocia took on that responsibility completely. There were changes she agreed with and changes she did not agree with, and her decisions stood. More significant, both she and I shared a deep commitment to the need to protect the rich orality of the narratives Henry and Barney had translated from Crow to English. Again and again, Phenocia would consider some question I had raised or additional wording I had suggested, and she would find the phrasing that fit both the Crow ear and the need for narrative clarification. There were times when my ignorance of Crow life ways distressed her, but she would work to communicate what was not understood and, in doing so, enhanced the text with sentences and footnotes here or there that were more lucid, more appropriate in tone and word than, I believe, those that anyone else could have written. Phenocia also is responsible for combining and organizing the explanations of Crow life in chapter 1 that were scattered throughout the original four texts. It also was entirely her innovation to restructure the song lyrics into verse format. Phenocia has worked hard to create a text that will read well. To that end, she has made judicious editorial decisions throughout, but always, foremost in her mind, has been the oral and cultural integrity of the manuscripts in front of her. Our heart concern has been to edit in such a way that our work merited Barney's approval and blessing.

Although I was the professor in this situation, I have been awed by, and taught by, my student as we read and reread the manuscripts to be sure that what you will read honors the original tellers of these tales, the men who have passed them down from decade to decade, especially Henry and Barney Old Coyote, who were entrusted to translate the stories from Crow to English. As you read these tales, you will both complete an oral exchange and keep it ongoing.

Alanna Kathleen Brown

When named, I was called *Baa Aatchilaho,* "Things of Good Fortune Are Hers." Time would verify and validate what a true and good name I had been given by Joseph Medicine Crow, my Whistle Water clan papa. My fathers started me on a privileged path early.

I was born to a Winnebago mother, the former Clara Tebo, and a Crow father, Barney Old Coyote Jr. The life ways in which I was raised mostly reflected the Crow traditions. Within the Crow kinship system my father's brothers are my papas, so I was fortunate to have many papas who cared about me and were willing to share their insights and knowledge. Whether we lived on the Crow reservation or elsewhere, times spent with family were always rich with influences and exposure to the wealth of wisdom and experiences of these people. Stories were told and we listened. These same stories have been passed down from one generation to the next. As a child and young adult I assumed that most Crows had these same stories told to them, that they also knew the background stories of the Crow people, the origins of ceremonies, and sites that figure prominently in our people's history.

I was extremely fortunate to have known my father's mother until her crossing over to the other camp at the age of 106. As a young adult I began to realize the wealth she had conveyed to her children and subsequently to their children, and to the generations that have followed. She was a product of the oral tradition that has sustained our people from the beginning. It was through her and her parents, her husband and his parents, that their children gained respect for and understanding of who they were and where they came from. They were the current conveyers of the future. They had been attentive, had learned the appropriate ways in which stories were told and rituals conducted, all the unseen nuances that were instrumental in the perpetuation of the culture. She was their touchstone.

As time progressed, I began to realize that my papas were more special than I understood. Their experiences set them apart. I learned that on 7 December 1941, when my seventeen-year-old father heard of the bombing at Pearl Harbor, he enlisted. His older brother Henry, "Hank," nine years his senior, in a brotherly fashion and in the Crow tradition, accompanied his younger brother to war. Their experiences together are legendary. They were a team; they practiced Crow ways even in foreign environments, as warriors and as brothers.

Their successful return home from the war was an event. They were treated as heroes, yet they remembered their big brothers with gifts from their battles. Not every enlisted Army Air Corpsman had flown with General Doolittle in the European theater. Nor had every mother gotten letters from General Hap Arnold responding to her plea that her sons be allowed to remain together in the military, contrary to policy. He maintained written contact with my grandmother to keep her updated about the whereabouts of her sons. Not every child was fortunate enough to hear stories of camaraderie and success from papas, as I did. In their stories of far-off places, they spoke of the varieties of cultures they encountered, as well as the rigors of being gunners on B-17 bombers in Europe, North Africa, and in the Mediterranean. I remain grateful that my fathers had gone to war in December 1941 and returned safely in June 1945.

The Old Coyote brothers returned home from the military highly decorated with both combat and noncombat medals, including the Air Medal with oak clusters, the Silver Star with cluster, Campaign Medals, and several Battle Stars. Barney, an expert marksman, was listed in the *Stars and Stripes* magazine as a recipient of the Soldiers Medal. These prestigious honors were important not only in the military but to the Crow people. My Crow name was in fact bestowed after Joseph Medicine Crow recounted his wartime deeds. His acknowledgment of good fortune in surviving battle situations unscathed was the inspiration.

There were other battles to be fought when the brothers returned. The survival of a young family in the economically depressed area was a priority. In the early 1950s, however, I didn't know that we were poor or that my family struggled financially. What I did know is that I had had a rich childhood. There were so many people who cared about me. They shared with me, they nursed me, they corrected and guided me. "Has Good Fortune" was truly an appropriate name for me.

My father began a full-time career with the U.S. government in 1949. We were stationed in different locations, as were military families. Wherever my family lived when I was a young child, memories of my uncle and father are tied to those places. Several times, we lived among tribes that, according to the stories I had heard, were historically "enemies." Yet my memories of those places and people are of respect both given and received by my fathers. They shared stories with the old-timers in these places, and as a result their tales were enhanced by "hearing the other side." They honored the past and brought it to the present.

In 1964, when my father's work took us to the arenas of Washington DC, his brother was still, as ever, his confidant, his consultant. My father began as a special assistant to the secretary of the Interior, appointed to that position by then President Lyndon Baines Johnson. We had arrived at the place our forefathers recognized as the place where decisions were made, policies determined. My fathers were a part of this process: they testified before congressional hearings (both are quoted in congressional records), and they knew the policy makers on a first-name basis. They helped to determine indigenous peoples' rights and to make them policy. The brothers were in the forefront of the American Indian Religious Freedom Act. Entering into this battle in 1973, they rejoiced in 1978 when Public Law 93-341 was enacted. In this same period, my father also challenged the government's recognition of the Native American Church and won his landmark tax case, *Barney Old Coyote vs. Director, Internal Revenue Service*, in U.S. court. The Old Coyote brothers wrote speeches, their opinions were sought. These important people were my fathers. They proved to their brothers, to their own children, and to Native people that it is possible to help steer the course of destiny. They were eloquent in their simple and passionate approach and they were heard.

Their involvement in all levels of presentation and preservation of culture kept them busy and visible. My papa Hank attended a gathering of Native peoples from around the country to share their respective practices and cultures. From this gathering came a book, *Respect for Life*. Lifelong friends were made at this conference; these cultural historians from Indian country were part of my fathers' increasing wealth of cultural knowledge.

When my father retired from government service, he had other irons in the fire. His desire to bring recognition to Native people was again evidenced by his work to get the Native population recognized at various levels. He was awarded an Honorary Doctorate in Humane Letters from Montana State University, Bozeman, Montana, in 1968. Using this calling card, he worked to get the Native American Studies Program started in 1970 at Montana State. Until this time, Native students were part of the Foreign Student Program; the separation acknowledged the population's unique and rich heritage. The programs and classes initiated were integrated with other departments and their respective curricula.

The family was back on home territory, within a day's drive of the Crow reservation. But my father's dedication to furthering his people still wasn't complete. Within a few years of getting the Montana State University Native American Studies Program up and running, the wheels were again in motion. Since economic development for Native Americans on reservations was basically nonexistent, he worked on the formation of the American Indian National Bank in 1972, a laborious and time-consuming project. He commuted to Washington DC to be the bank's president and chairman of the board. By the early 1970s, he was easily a member of an airline's Million-Mile Club. His ability and familiarity with international finance houses and their prestigious personnel amounted to another coup. In 1973 the American Indian National Bank was chartered. This monumental event included the efforts of two federal departments. The Department of Commerce and its two agencies, the Office of Minority Business (OMB) and the Economic Development Agency (EDA), as well as the Department of the Interior and its agency, the Bureau of Indian Affairs (BIA), helped to bring this dream to fruition.

When my father returned to Montana to continue the upbringing of my four young siblings upon the death of our mother, his wife of thirty-three years, his work was frequently more localized. While Barney consulted around the country, his brother and sister-in-law, Stella, went to Washington DC. Henry was the cultural specialist for the Select Senate Committee on Indian Affairs, and the voice of sense and purpose of the Old Coyote brothers was still present in the decision-making arenas.

Whenever the brothers got together, their attention was drawn back to tape recordings of stories they had begun years previous. They continued compiling their information, striving for accuracy and authenticity and following the Crow way of story presentation. Before Hank's crossing over in 1988, the brothers had collaborated to compile the four stories that follow. After the death of his lifelong companion, friend, and confidant, my father continued to work on their dream. His battles were now with technology: word-processing machines had replaced laborious typewriters but were rife with crashes, programs "blowing up," or material disappearing. Learning new skills and facing frequent frustrations, Dad persevered.

More recognition was to come for the brothers. In 1988, ten days after burying Henry, Dad was notified that he and his brother were corecipients of a prestigious honor at the Smithsonian Institute of Space and Aeronautics for their deeds during World War II. With a heavy heart, he went to Washington DC without his brother to accept their award. This National Service Award, bestowed by the Vietnam Veterans Coalition, was authorized by Congress and accompanied by a medal struck by the U.S. Mint. As recently as 30 November 1999, Barney's warrior spirit was still being honored. As an invited guest of the secretary of the army, he delivered a keynote address at the Pentagon. President Bill Clinton had declared November "National American Indian Heritage Month" to honor American Indians in the military. My father is currently designated designer/consultant in the Pentagon's Memorial to American Indian Veterans.

Passion, commitment, and dedication to the perseverance of a culture and the perpetuation of life ways are necessary to a people's sense of identity. We need to know where we came from to understand who we are. My fathers, all of them, have instilled this in their children. We are fortunate that they chose to listen, cared enough to share, and went one step further, preserving on tape and paper the efforts of their work. Their taped sessions, the songs, the stories are a wonderful gift to those who remember their voices, young, confident, and strong. For those who may not remember those young men, the sound of elders' voices recounting a people's story is heartening and empowering.

That my own children, born of Crow and Winnebago background on their mother's side and German and Norwegian heritage on their father's side, would treasure the works of their grandpas is a gift. The time my children have chosen to spend in the company of their grandfather is a blessing. They all love to be his driver on his frequent road trips. They have their own historical and cultural resource in the beloved stories. Phenocia, *Ak Ikkaa Aho,* thank you for yet another confirmation that my name is a good name, a true name; indeed, I still enjoy "good fortune." You are continuing a tradition that has sustained our people for generations. Your sisters and brothers, my grandchildren, and many others unknown to us will benefit from your efforts.

Aho,
Patricia Old Coyote Bauerle

I am a product of multiple worldviews and a combination of different cultures. I was raised with the predominant Western worldview, but I was also instilled with the traditions of my Native American roots. Lately I find myself looking more deeply into what it means to be of mixed blood. I am of two worlds and have always moved within and between both, somewhat oblivious to their different methods of understanding, communicating, and forming identity. Recently I have felt the need to ground myself more thoroughly in my Crow heritage. I have sought the stories that would unite me with the past, forming a living connection.

My involvement with this book began as an undergraduate research project on Crow literature. I expected to examine the identity of my people, the Crows, but a more complex and intimate understanding of my own identity has blossomed as well. In reading stories that have come from my people, I found a rich source for understanding the history that surrounds my tribe; the words connect me with the many who have come before. I am a fifth-generation descendent of Mountain Chief (Piegan), a sixth-generation descendent of the great Crow chief Sits in the Middle of the Land. My great-great-grandfather Old Coyote was a well respected man among many tribes, and my great-grandfather Barney Old Coyote Sr. was a renowned trick rider, performer, and orator. His wife, Mae Takes the Gun Old Coyote Childs, was an accomplished leader in many arenas in her lifetime. My grandfather Barney Old Coyote Jr. has also made a name for himself as a warrior, an educator, a businessman, a leader, and a historian. Still, the connection between these names and me was somewhat obscured by the Western perspective of history being confined to the past. I was caught somewhere between being Crow and being Anglo.

I was fortunate enough to grow up with the advantages of being acclimated to both worlds. My father is of German and Norwegian descent. He grew up in New York, which is two thousand miles from my mother's origins in Montana. I was raised just off the Crow reservation, in a small college town whose population fluctuates by eleven thousand people between summer and the school year. It is a predominantly Anglo community, so I have had the standard Westernized worldview education. My parents took the time and care to instill the traditional beliefs of the Crows in my siblings and me so that we might understand where we as individuals are coming from and how that impacts who we are. Both my parents practice and believe in the traditions of the Crows, even though my father is not of the same ethnic background as my mother. My father sees something that moves him in the belief system and practices of my mother's tribe, so over the years he has been accepted and become a part of the culture, as the culture has also become a part of him. Because of our parents' shared beliefs, the identities of me and my siblings have been strongly influenced by Crow traditions.

Western and Native views of identity differ greatly. From a Western standpoint, we believe that we shape our own identity, for the most part. We define who we are by how we want others to perceive us. Although we link ourselves to family, in Western society the individual is valued above all else. From a Native view, the individual is important, but he or she is unquestionably tied to the whole and to family. Put another way, the individual's identity is recognizably shaped by his or her roots. This is not to say that other worldviews do not draw influence from family and cultural history, but I believe that there is something unique about Native worldviews because identity is kept alive and carried along through the story of the people.

The oral tradition is a system of knowledge that has been used by Native peoples for millennia. It instructs and preserves cultural life ways for Native peoples throughout the world. It is the key to the past, present, and future. Traditional stories have been told to teach morals, the rewards and unwanted consequences of actions, and the importance of self-discipline and integrity, all through example. Illustrating this, Native American stories have also passed down family and tribal history, which differs from Western fiction and folk tales, whose primary function is entertainment. Because it has been relatively recently that the written word has found a firm place within Native communities, the oral tradition has survived through the present as the living link to history. Each story that is told by grandparents and parents has been passed down through generations of family with the intention of maintaining the members' identity as a people. Each detail is important in a particular way to convey a worldview supported by the account. For these reasons, there is an amazingly accurate and complex historical record within native peoples' oral cultures that is at once very delicate and culturally grounded.

The notion of identity from a Native standpoint stems from the family as follows. When I introduce myself as the great-great-granddaughter of Old Coyote, Crows have knowledge of my family and therefore know of my background and of me. This concept not only lends itself to families that are aware of members and kinship ties, but also lends necessity to knowledge of family history. Because family is such an essential component of individual identity, the individual must also know the expectations that come with being the descendent of a person who has earned honor and prestige. The honor is passed along to the descendant, but so is the expectation that the ancestor's integrity will be maintained and not blemished. With story, life ways and expectations continue to be passed down.

As an English major who has turned to the few existing texts that deal with my people, I have come across many difficult issues. The majority of the materials that exist are autobiographies cowritten by anthropologists, interviews by historians, and historical accounts of the Crows written by Euroamerican scholars. Many of these pieces do offer a link to the past of the Crow people through retold and translated accounts of individuals' lives. What these texts lack is the attention to detail of the oral tradition. The Crow people have fashioned guidelines to ensure the preservation of story. One of these guidelines is that stories have more than one version because there are many perceptions of a single event. If multiple people witnessed an event, it would be recounted from a collective viewpoint, with each witness adding his or her own perspective to get an accurate picture. If the event did not have eyewitnesses, those who had heard the story from someone else would tell their versions and reach a consensus. This is where the details of a story remaining intact are important. Generally, a person being told a story can trace the progression of the story back to its original tellers. The sharing of the story by the new recipient should then be carried out accurately, lest it reflect poorly on every person who has told the story before. The belief that everything is interconnected and related and has an impact on everything else extends to all areas of life, and here is where the problems that I have encountered with texts about my people come into play. The majority of the texts I have read are not written with the care found in Crow oral tradition. The Western worldview, which involves a tendency to overanalyze, to see events as black and white, interferes with the Native worldview of interconnectedness and the understanding of how and why things are done.

Many Native authors have illustrated this difference in their contemporary writing—Leslie Marmon Silko, Scott Momaday, Joy Harjo, and Mary Tallmountain, for example. Still, very little exists in terms of traditional oral stories that have been preserved and passed down with the care that the oral tradition demands, and in turn which continue to preserve and perpetuate a particular way of life. The contrast between Western and Native perceptions of reality has complicated the process of recording Native stories and experiences in the written form. For instance, the Western tendency to seek understanding through questioning differs greatly from the Native tendency to seek understanding through observation. The Western scientific process, which progresses in a linear fashion, teaches us that we may answer a question through inquiry, while a Native approach to answering a question is to examine the world around us, looking at the times that have come before and those that will come after and deciding how the present fits into the big picture. The moment in which an event happens is not always the most important time to examine. If a non-Native interviewer is unaware of these concepts, and he or she interviews a Native who is equally unfamiliar with the Western process of inquiry, the probability is high that many details important to fully understanding the significance of seemingly minor events or actions will go unexplained. For the full meaning and significance of a traditional story to be conveyed, someone with a deep understanding of the culture from which it comes must present it. This understanding is not one that comes with living near another culture, or even living among its people to study the culture; rather, it comes from a person who lives the culture and recognizes the nuances and symbolism that a story contains.

The lack of Native peoples speaking for themselves is owing to many causes and has resulted in the misinterpretation and false representation of many things. Early on, the problem of translation interfered with people's basic ability to communicate with those outside their cultural sphere. To illustrate, the writing of *Black Elk Speaks* was translated by one party, then transcribed in shorthand, which was later rewritten to make up the original transcript. The possibility for errors is staggering. The failure of Anglo people to comprehend Native worldviews (and vice versa) has resulted in false assumptions, omitted details, and skewed interpretations.

In the two-fold process of translation, the verbal or physical act of translating from one language to another is accompanied by the theoretical or mental translation of meaning from one worldview to another. This process creates a problem for many texts that are based on interviews of Native peoples by non-Natives. Translating the worldview of a culture is a difficult process that is often inhibited by the translator's inability to surrender his or her own worldview to truly understand a different culture. People consider themselves fluent in a foreign language once they begin to think in that language; this is the kind of transformation non-Native writers must experience, beginning to think in another culture.

It is on this point that my own identity becomes important in relation to the broader identity of a culture. Because I have grown out of both the colonizers and the colonized, I have come to understand both worlds; such dual understanding did not come into full bloom until my generation.

The appreciation of both Native and Western worldviews allows for a more accurate translation on both levels, as the story that is communicated is not explained by someone from outside of the culture who is speculating based on research rather than experience.

Autobiography is a European genre and is foreign to Crow tradition. In my upbringing it was taught that bragging or placing importance of self over others is improper. If one's life is extraordinary, others will notice and pass on his or her stories. It is not the individual's place to decide that his or her actions are righteous enough to be celebrated. This belief keeps Native peoples humble.

Frank B. Linderman, a writer in the late 1920s and early 1930s, employed autobiography in *Plenty-coups, Chief of the Crows* and *Pretty Shield: Medicine Woman of the Crows* to record the lives of two figures in the Crow tribe. Linderman grew up in Montana among the Crows and recognized the importance of recording the life stories of important people during a period of drastic lifestyle changes for Native peoples. He modified the European genre to be more accepting of Crow traditions by incorporating oral story-telling presentations. In his first book, Linderman describes Plenty Coups telling his story with two other men who had shared many experiences by his side. In noting the manner in which Plenty Coups recounts his stories, Linderman does what many writers do not in their autobiographies and biographies of Crow people: he keeps the story as true as possible by acknowledging the multiple accounts he hears. Whether or not Linderman actually recognized the process that he was witnessing as an integral component of the oral tradition, he did acknowledge it. Traditionally the other people present during a storytelling verify or discredit the story so that the truth is told. This method ensures that the tale, which is such a large component of identity, remains intact. By contrast, the tendency of non-Native authors and editors to find a single source for information (be it an individual or only one family) invites the possibility of distortions and inaccuracies.

The Crows' careful process of story preservation makes sense when one understands the tales' importance. I need to emphasize that the stories in this volume and others like them are not merely historical accounts of events in the Crow tribe, or of family members. The narratives tell where it is that people come from, and they are therefore just as much a part of the present as the past. I myself have had to come to this realization. The vast

xxi

amount of knowledge that I inherited about my people, told to me by my grandfather on our drives through the two hundred miles of land between the reservation and where my family lives in Bozeman, at first registered simply as history. I always cherished the stories, but being educated in white schools, I initially failed to see how important such stories are to my own identity. What is history from a Western viewpoint is an integral part of selfhood from a Native viewpoint. To illustrate further, when my great-grandmother was born in 1890, her first Indian name, Strikes Coup on the Ice, was in reference to one of the battles that is discussed in the following text. Her identity was entwined with Crow history.

The land where stories take place is a very important component of the Crows' oral tradition. As these stories link my people to ancestors and tribal history, the tales also link us to our original homeland. Native American tribes around the country have similar creation stories, but they all differ slightly according to the geography of their homelands. Because the land is what sustained people for millennia, there are very close ties to the land from which the stories originated. This land-specific quality becomes as much a part of the identity of the people as story is, because the narratives are inseparable from the lands where they were born. I am amazed as I drive down the highway now, thinking of events that are directly related to me even though they happened a hundred years ago. Each member of the Crow tribe shares this connection to our homeland; these stories are part of the Crows' legacy.

The Way of the Warrior: Stories of the Crow People is the most accurate translation of the oral tradition into written word that I have ever read. This is perhaps the first Crow text to thoroughly bridge the communication gap between two cultures. The Old Coyote brothers' detailed explanations of things for the benefit of outsiders demonstrates their awareness of misunderstandings between Native and Western cultures. For those without a full understanding of the background of the Crows, my great-grandfathers embedded in the stories explanations of terms that have potential for mistranslation. Their asides appear in brackets. True to the form of the oral tradition, these stories speak to the reader directly to engage him or her in the narrative.

The process of compiling these stories began during 1955 and 1956 in response to false representations of many traditions and stories. Henry Old Coyote began to search for the multiple versions of stories that he knew existed in order to get the truest representation of particular events, traditions, and physical sites. He traveled all over Montana, compiling different accounts from the Assinaboine and Piegan tribes, among others. Henry founded the Culture Commission of the Crow tribe to help with his work, funding the research and recordings through the Crow tribe itself. To maintain the method of hearing multiple accounts while gathering information, Henry sought the input of each of the six districts in the Crow tribe (which are based on the clans of the Crows). The information recorded included battle sites and stories of Crow heroes stretching all the way into the pre-reservation period, when Crow delegates traveled to Washington DC. Larry Lowendorf, an archeologist and anthropologist from the University of Missouri, helped catalog and explore the field sites that Henry was researching, so a veritable gold mine of information regarding Crow history and traditions now exists. Henry's brothers, Barney Old Coyote Jr. and Joseph Medicine Crow, acted as compilers of the information. After Henry quit working as a liaison for the Culture Commission, he continued to research and record information relating to the history and traditions of the Crow tribe. This is when the two brothers, Henry and Barney, came to translate the stories included in this text from Crow into English.

These accounts greatly honor the oral tradition in both the inclusion of multiple voices and the clarity of detail. Details within the oral tradition are the small pieces of a story that reinforce cultural beliefs and practices and guide listeners to the exact place where the recounted events took place. (Directions are worked right into the narration, so one could visit original sites if so inclined.) Each of the stories in this collection is a classic example of the place that the oral tradition occupies within the Crow culture. These are stories of warriors who were the epitome of what was considered great in a leader and a man. Each story illustrates morals and beliefs that are essential to the traditions of the Crows. "The Saga of Red Bear" shows how bravery is rewarded and praised, and the importance of thinking of the honor of others over one's personal desires. "The Story of Spotted Horse" illustrates the difficulties of being different and a method of overcoming them, while showing the rewards of bravery and perseverance. This story also tells how Spotted Horse gained his name, revealing the complexity of the oral tradition and the social structure of the Crows.

The importance of story to Native cultures cannot be overemphasized. In the telling, a cultural worldview is passed along as well. The ability for members of the tribe to see what made a Crow hero great is as important now as it was centuries ago. While some themes, such as the ways of a nomadic lifestyle and the practice of war, are not as crucial as they were in the past, the stories nevertheless bear important messages about how we are to lead our lives. The tales illustrate how an individual is made through his efforts, how the struggle of a man to become something great can be worthwhile, and how reputation and glory can disappear if individuals lose sight of their place within society. Because these stories were born of oral tradition, which thrives on interpretation, they can be easily adapted to fit contemporary situations, told and retold in ways that focus on specific events for the moral effect that is desired. "Remember Spotted Horse, remember Hunts to Die," the storyteller can say, "and do not lose sight of who you are for what you believe yourself to be." In this way, these stories are as valuable to the Crow people today as they were two hundred years ago.

The preparation of this preface material was carried out with as much care as were the narratives, for this multivoice introduction is a key part of the traditional Crow communication process. Dr. Alanna Kathleen Brown, Patricia Bauerle, and I offer unique perspectives on this work, as we each played a role in developing it. This threefold viewpoint extends the custom from which these stories came.

I wish to thank the numerous people who encouraged and supported my efforts on this project: Dr. Alanna Kathleen Brown for her involvement in and commitment to the text; the English Department of Montana State University for its continued support; Dr. Alexandra New Holy; and my family, especially my grandfathers and grandmothers, who have helped me to realize the importance of these cultural teachings and traditions, and what it is to be Crow. I invite you and all the readers to share these stories that are part of me, part of the authors, and part of all the Crow people. In doing so, you will be perpetuating the oral tradition of passing stories down to children and grandchildren.

Aho,
Phenocia Bauerle

The Way of the Warrior

MONTANA

WYOMING

BLACK HILLS

Milk River

Missouri River

Musselshell River

Elk River

Tongue River

Powder River

Little Powder River

Big Horn River

Little Big Horn River

Shoshone River

Wind River

Yellowstone Lake

Madison R.

Jefferson R.

Gallatin R.

Big Hole R.

① Mission Creek, Montana
② Where Red Bear Camped
③ Splintered End's Camp
④ Where Spotted Horse Fought
⑤ Dragon's Mouth–Fringe's Father
⑥ Where *Shee-she* and Red Bear
  Fought against the Sioux

● - - ● The "four teepee poles" Chief Sits in the
      Middle of the Land designated as "Crow Country"

✕ - - ✕ "Crow Country" as translated by the
      Ft. Laramie Friendship Treaty of 1851

N

Crow Country

PART I

The Crow Way of Life

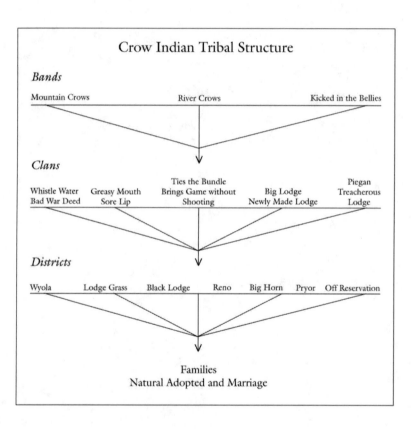

Crow Indian Tribal Structure

Bands

Mountain Crows   River Crows   Kicked in the Bellies

Clans

| Whistle Water | Greasy Mouth | Ties the Bundle Brings Game without Shooting | Big Lodge Newly Made Lodge | Piegan Treacherous |
| Bad War Deed | Sore Lip | | | Lodge |

Districts

Wyola   Lodge Grass   Black Lodge   Reno   Big Horn   Pryor   Off Reservation

Families
Natural Adopted and Marriage

The Crow Community
through Changing Times

The Crow Nation has experienced many changes throughout history, but it has maintained strength in community in a way unique to this country and in the history of Indian tribes. This discussion focuses on some aspects of that community through change after change.[1]

BACKGROUND

The Crow Nation resides in southeastern Montana on a reservation established through a series of treaties and legislation beginning in 1851 with the Treaty of Ft. Laramie. Tribal members number just under ten thousand, with over half the tribal population living on or near the reservation, with their headquarters in Crow Agency, Montana. Reservation lands range from lofty mountain divides to lush foothills to the semiarid lands of the northern plains. When the present boundaries of the reservation were established by the 1920 Crow Act, the tribe conveyed certain lands to the State of Montana in return for public schools on the reservation. U.S. government schools on the reservation were discontinued at that time, and this was also the last time that tribal lands were allotted among tribal members.

The Crow language is linguistically classified as Siouan. Hostilities before reservation life existed with practically all neighboring tribes except the Hidatsas of North Dakota, the parent tribe of the Crows. History records that the Crows have always been friendly with the Anglos, beginning with the 1825 Friendship Treaty.

The Crow people have strong ties to their homeland, Crow Country. The people originally lived in caves, then evolved into teepee dwellers.

3

Some evidence suggests that they were agrarian before becoming buffalo hunters of the plains. Crows were renowned as horsemen on the frontier and had used dogs as beasts of burden before the arrival of horses. The physical relationship between Crows and their land extends through the tribe's historic, legendary, and ancient past. Unlike some other tribes, which have reservation lands not of their choosing, the Crows have always regarded their present location as Crow Country—to be protected, cherished, and preserved as their home even if there be only one Crow left (paraphrased from Sits in the Middle of the Land, principal chief of the Crows, Ft. Laramie Treaty, 1868).

Tribal members are tradition oriented and identify with other members through clan and values systems tempered by the land and environment of Crow Country. The values system has been influenced by other characteristics of the tribe, but the essential strength of the tribe has been a precisely defined clan system, which remains intact to this day. From time to time, this system has been augmented by militaristic and other related practices.

The Crows continue to look to the development of their land and resources as a way to maintain a perpetual home. The tribe conducts official business through a general council of all members that are of voting age. The tribe elects four principal officers—chairman, vice chairman, secretary, and vice secretary—and a number of commission and committee members. Veto and other powers rest with the general council as in days past. The "chief system" was discontinued following the demise of the last traditional chief, Plenty Coups, in 1932.

The Crows now have a written language, developed in the 1960s and 1970s, although it is not in general use in the written form by members of the tribe. It is taught in the schools on the reservation and in a few in-state colleges, particularly at the Crow tribal college, Little Big Horn College. The extensive oral tradition has been kept intact by the tribe in spite of a considerable decrease in Crow-speaking members in the recent past.

THE CROW CLAN SYSTEM TODAY

The Crow clan system is built on the premise that there is strength in family. The system extends family beyond parents and siblings, carrying those relationships into a complex but highly functional structure. Identification within the tribe is through a matrilineal system. Children belong to the clan

4

of their birth mother and are related to all members of that clan. In keeping with the tribal practice of having only parent, sibling, and grandparent roles, all tribal members younger than the mother are brothers and sisters. Women of the same clan who are older than the mother are mothers. Crow has no word for aunt, uncle, cousin, nephew, or niece.

The Crow tribe originally had thirteen clans. Today, ten of the original clans remain. The dissipation happened in the 1860s and 1870s, finally leaving ten clans in 1884. These ten are paired into five groupings, like sister clans (see the diagram on page 2). They are defined by districts of the reservation where they have typically lived, but are formally related to each other. Relations (e.g., sisters and brothers) extend across clan lines within the groupings of sister clans. The clan structure works directly with the kinship system of the Crows, allowing for an extended family system. The system makes it possible for an individual to have multiple parents, grandparents, siblings, and other relatives within the clan to turn to for guidance and support. It is taboo for two people of the same clan to marry, preventing bloodlines from becoming too intermixed.

Identity and personality are directly related to clanship. Characteristics of individuals are frequently attributed to clan tendencies, such as being clever or simple minded or having a good singing voice. Individuals' worth and prestige are also considered related to their clan. Each clan has its own traditional honor and praise songs, giving substance to the belief that the songs originated from a greater power that blessed the clans in different ways. Friendly rivalry exists among the clans: contests have been held to determine which is the most accomplished. These contests, extending from the traditional to the contemporary, from tribal activities to non-Indian pursuits, include games such as hand-game and arrows.

PRESENT ACTIVE CLANS

Outside of intermarriage, the ten clans with their five groupings comprise the basic method of belonging to the Crow tribe. The clan system governs all manners of identification and fellowship and leads to loyalty and support among its members.

Newly Made Lodge and Big Lodge

Some time after the clans were established by First Maker and names given, the Newly Made Lodge was found to exist and named accordingly. Members of the Big Lodge were said to be husky.

Whistle Water and Bad War Deed

Whistle Water was originally known as Good Prairie Dogs. Incest was taboo within the tribe, hence it was improper for brothers and sisters to marry, even outside the immediate family and among members of the same clan who were not related by blood. It is told that members of this clan married within the clan, and while one man was courting a woman of his clan, he called to her by whistling while she was getting water. When he was confronted about whistling to her, he claimed that it was the water that made the whistling noise. The name of the clan was changed as a result.

The Bad War Deed clan is so named as a result of its bringing back fake war trophies.

Greasy Mouth and Sore Lip or Burned Lip

Members of the Greasy Mouth clan were excellent hunters and always seemed to enjoy the prime (fatty) parts of their game. Burned Lip clan members were not so accomplished in the art of hunting. Because they seemed to be out on the hunt and exposed to the elements for long periods, their lips were chapped, or "burned."

Piegan and Treacherous Lodge

The Piegan and Treacherous Lodge were sister clans that waged war with another clan of the tribe, the Whistle Water. The name identifies them as the enemy, the Piegans, traditional enemy of the Crows, suggesting that they are just as treacherous.

Ties the Bundle (Filth Eating Clan) and Brings Game without Shooting

Ties the Bundle gained its name because of the sloppy manner with which the members transported belongings in the nomadic way of life. It is told that an unfaithful woman was punished by being made to eat food not properly cleaned, spawning the clan's second name.

Brings Game without Shooting was named for its ability to bring back plentiful meat from game caught in ice jams and snowdrifts.

THE PATERNAL CLAN SYSTEM

Clan identification extends also to the children of male members of a clan, called "Clan Children" or "Teasing Clan." All children of male members of a clan identify with one another as brothers and sisters. Respect, teasing, tenderness, and all manners of relationships are governed by clan identification. Through this identification, members can tease, jest, and otherwise be overly critical of other members with impunity. Under the watchful eye of the brothers and sisters, an individual needs to conduct himself or herself with utmost care. This system results in a very effective self-control device.

OTHER METHODS OF IDENTIFICATION

In its history, the Crow tribe has enjoyed several methods of identification and function for members, but none has served tribal strength as long or as effectively as the clan system. Systems to identify tribal members have included the following.

Bands

After their separation from the parent tribe, the Hidatsas, the Crows were in three bands: the Mountain Crows (main camp), the River Crows, and the Kicked in the Bellies. This identification was diluted and became ineffective following the establishment of the Crow reservation in the Treaty of 1868. Before the treaty, the three bands functioned separately for the majority of the year. The lifestyle of plains Indians called for smaller groupings within the tribe so that travel and hunting would be more efficient. However, there was regular cross-traffic and frequent intermingling of band members.

Districts

Upon settling of the Crow reservation, from 1870 to 1890, six specific districts were established. This system was a dilution of the bands, but the districts remained as effective cross-sections of the clans. Contests and tribal committees continue to be based on the district system, but easy transportation and communication have effectively diluted the districts.

Today, many members of districts still identify with, but no longer live within, those districts and are members of an ever increasing entity called "off reservation." Those grouped into the off-reservation category still enjoy membership in tribal committees and contests.

GIVING HONOR

Among many practices and traditions of the Crows, honoring of heroes has been a key to tribal identification, function, and vitality. An example of this is an honor ceremony called the Dog Head Eating Ceremony, which is held in connection with a ceremonial dance called Daytime Dance (because it is held only during daylight). The detailed ceremony is complete with officers of the dance (War Dance) society, specific songs, and rituals. The Dog Head Eating Ceremony is a series of complex rituals culminating in honoring outstanding heroes of the tribe. The honorees usually number four and are anxiously anticipated because they will dramatically recount their respective deeds and accomplishments.

The ceremony came from tribes east of the Crows—the Omahas, Sioux, and Hidatsas. The Crows do not eat dogs, but because of the high honor of the ceremony among the tribes, the title Dog Head Eating has been retained. In days past, war heroes were honored in the ceremony, including veterans of World Wars I and II and other military conflicts in which Crows have been involved.

Since the establishment of reservations and the ending of intertribal warfare, give-aways have served as honor-bestowing ceremonies. They were implemented as education and employment accomplishments became sources of honor. In recent years, basketball has generated the excitement and interest of the Crows in an unprecedented and broad-sweeping fervor.

In 1997 the Hardin Bulldogs won the Montana State Class A Basketball Championship. The head coach was a Crow Indian, as were eight of the team members, along with the team manager and assistant coach. It was a great day for the Crows. Two weeks after the championship, the Crow tribe held a victory dance of three days to honor the Hardin Bulldogs, including the three non-Indians on the team. A feature of the celebration was the Dog Head Eating ceremony in which members of the winning team were honored in a ceremony as ancient as the Daytime Dance itself. An integral part of the 1997 ceremony was the name giving, the identification by clans and the perpetuation of the Crow ethic and vitality through the clan system.

Crow Values in the Stories

Stories of the Crow tribe are readily categorized into three basic periods: the ancient, the legendary, and the historical. Stories from the ancient period include those genesis stories that entail the origins of people and places, and in which all things animate and inanimate talk. The legendary period chronicles human exploits that gain legendary proportions as they are told and retold over time. The historical period consists of stories of events that have happened recently enough to be told as memoirs of great leaders and outstanding members of the tribe. These stories have several important characteristics. First, an ever present element of mysticism threads and weaves its way throughout the accounts. There is an adage that says, "Nothing is done simply," meaning that if one does not have the appropriate background or make adequate preparation, the difficult and impossible should not be attempted. Conversely, when one attempts a major undertaking, it is assumed that he or she has prepared well and has a true direction and success-oriented approach. Particularly, one must have the mystical and supernatural powers to attain predetermined goals and objectives, no matter how difficult. The Crows call this preparation having "backup," not doing things on a whim.

A second significant element in Crow stories is the portrayal of prestige and worthiness to be gained from the accomplishment of deeds. This is to say that those things that are held as most important to the tribe are reflected in the narratives. Foremost of these among men is the accomplishment of deeds leading to "chieftainship." A chief gains that stature in a manner similar to gaining a college degree today. A warrior would endeavor to become a chief and be very accomplished, but until he completed the requirements for chieftainship, he would not be considered for that position of leadership, prestige, and honor. Without the credentials that led to chieftainship, an individual could not assert himself as a leader, although he may have frequently been called upon to serve the chiefs.

A chief was above the "great men," "real men," "pipe carriers," and other distinguished men of the tribe. In the Crow language, the word chief *(batchet-che)* simply meant a "good man," a name and role that all young men of the tribe aspired to, trained for, and worked toward throughout their lifetime. Opportunities for completing the required deeds were rare. Requirements for becoming a "chief" were several, but the following usually were common.

First to strike the enemy in battle. This was the most prestigious of all the deeds and was used in deciding whether battles were victories or defeats. A victorious homecoming featured the "striker of coup" as the principal hero who was afforded the honor of "leading the procession" (as the victorious war party ran or galloped through the camp). This honor could occur several times in a single battle ("second to strike" and so on).

First to strike the camp. This deed involved "touching the enemy's lodge" and other hazardous and precarious tasks as determined by the war party. The deeds were classified in descending order, with the first "striker" always number one.

Taking a weapon from the enemy in combat. This honor was high, as it signified a deft and daring maneuver performed in the heat of battle. After gunpowder came into use, the taking of a "metal gun" (rifle) from the enemy replaced in importance the simple taking of a weapon.

Taking an enemy's horse and bringing it home. The significance of this act was manifold. Of highest importance was the taking of a horse in battle. Almost equally important was the taking or stealthily cutting of a prized horse from its tether in front of the enemy's lodge. It was a frequent practice of Plains Indians and Crows to tether prized horses immediately in front of lodges so as to frustrate the enemy. The bringing of the enemy's horse(s) home to the camp was festive and regarded with great prestige. The importance of this act is reflected in names that commemorate and memorialize it: "Cuts the Horse in Front of the Lodge," "Brings Ten [Horses]," "Brings a Hundred," and "Goes on a Quest for a Painted Horse."

Leading a successful war party. This accomplishment was the culmination of the deeds required for chieftainship and could occur along with other required deeds in a single foray or incident. A war party leader was usually called the "war party chief" in recognition of having previously completed the other requirements. The word of the war party chief was law. He embodied the potential success or failure of the venture, and the role was one to be at once feared and cherished. It marked the person for the rest of his life. His mystical and supernatural powers, indeed, his "medicine," were all subject to open and critical scrutiny. The degree of his success was a measure of how the tribe and its members would rely upon him in the future.

Of highest prestige were war parties in which the objective was one supported by a significant majority of the tribe or band; the predetermined objectives of the war party were accomplished; the enemy was devastated, ravaged, and humiliated; there was minimal damage and loss to the war party; and the power (mystical and supernatural) and medicine of the leader was clearly demonstrated. When the foregoing were accomplished, a war-party chief was said to have "done things right," indicating that whatever powers he claimed or was said to possess were confirmed. Narratives of his exploits would be included among the legends and stories of the tribe to be remembered throughout the generations.

Crow stories often portray elements of the Crow way of life in a manner that indelibly imprints attributes of Crows upon the minds of the listener, forever perpetuating desirable values and principles. For instance, good people in Crow stories do not just become that way by themselves, or by their blood and upbringing; they have "backup," mystical or supernatural means of accomplishing their goals. A child becomes the object of good wishes, prayers, and mystical influences even before birth, sometimes even before conception. The stories' magical elements capture the imagination and ensure that the narratives live on through retelling, because they capture the essence of Crow beliefs.

MYSTICAL POWERS AND MEDICINE

According to Crow tradition, mystical powers (medicine) come from the great maker (God) through one or more of His creations. The creations of the Greater Power may be heavenly bodies, birds, animals, and other beings and objects both seen and unseen. Mystical powers or medicine can be vested in a mortal through a variety of visitations (revelations). A common practice for acquiring these supernatural powers is the process called the "vision quest." Individuals deprive themselves of human comforts, fasting and pleading to the spirit world in isolated hills or mountains or alongside waters. When successful, the revelation can be a dream during sleep, a message from the unknown, a vision during delirium, or an actual experience. Among the Crows, such a revelation is called a "dream." When people speak of such events, they might say, "He had a good dream," "His dream was true," or "His dream was what he wanted." When people are disposed to follow what they experienced from a revelation, they say things like, "I saw it in a dream," "I was shown that in a dream," or on rarer occasions, "I actually saw it as backup."

Dreams (in sleep or otherwise) play a major role in the lives of Crow people. Good wishes are parallel to dreams. Dreams and good wishes are shared among people as a means of portraying the future. If a person has dreams and wishes told for him and he accepts them, he makes it his goal to fulfill these and feels certain they will become true.

It might be said, "I saw a particular season. It was good. I will see that season with this person in good health and in good fortune." With that, the future is cast. Both the well-wisher and the subject then look to the future with good expectation. Wishes are also cast over longer periods and toward more specific goals. "I want this child to be a good person." "I want this person to be a good warrior." "I want this person to be healthy and wealthy." "I want this person to have a good home." "I wish for him a good education." The well-wisher or "dream teller" has a role like that of a godparent from then on.

In a dream, vision, or an actual experience (revelation), the recipient is blessed with powers bestowed through the grace of a Greater Power, manifest in something that is familiar. This could be the Morning Star, the Moon (old, old woman), the Sun (old, old man), or other creations, including beings from the bird and animal. So it is that there is bear medicine, bird medicine, and others. Sometimes, living beings dwell within a person and become a part of him or her, a constant companion and a source of mystical power. This is called *baachilape*. In the Red Bear story, Top of the Mountain saw several occasions in which powerful men painted themselves from within.

DESIRABLE QUALITIES

The Crow people held good men and women in high esteem. It was not enough to be attractive; one had to meet other demanding qualities to be counted as either a good woman or good man. A good woman was hard to find, a rare being to be sought and cherished. To be numbered as a good woman, one had to embody the following: attractiveness, physically and in personality; industriousness and accomplishment in the skills and arts of women; faithfulness and chastity; soundness and goodness as represented by evenness of disposition. Good women were patient, astute, and clever. They had good health, strength, and endurance and the ability to endure discomfort, pain, and suffering. They were accomplished in social skills such as singing, dancing, and manner of dress.

A good man was the core, life, and strength of the tribe. While both the male and female roles within the tribe were important, the lifestyle of the Crow people made it necessary for a man to be a good provider and warrior to ensure the survival of both the tribe and the family. A listing of a good man's qualities generally included the following: attractiveness, physically and in other ways; strength, speed afoot and great endurance; and possession of a good, loud voice. Such men were unattached to worldly things and were of an outgoing nature, showing kindness to tribal members, particularly the defenseless and poorer tribal members such as children and elders. Good men were good providers, accomplished in social skills such as singing and dancing. They excelled at all things physical, such as being a good marksman.

Good men did not cherish material things or lasting relationships. As the traditional saying goes, "Nothing is forever, only the sky and earth are forever. Glory endures." Hence, good men were not jealous or possessive of wives, family, or earthly things. Men who left wives or "threw them away" were often performing prestigious acts. They demonstrated how little they cared for temporal attachments. "Throwing away" a spouse (it could be done by either sex but was more frequent among men) acknowledged that one was so conscious of this principle that he or she would give up everything, even what was most dear. The act also illustrated the generosity of the individual, as he or she would most likely be giving away a prized "good woman" or "good man."

Many of these qualities are still used today in determining a "good man" or a "good woman." Another common measure of a good person is in the friends *(iilapaache)* that a person enjoys. The friendships a person has are but one measure of the goodness of that person. An undesirable person is characterized as "one without friends," "one who does not enjoy the good feelings or graces of others *(baawittasheleetak)*."

Among women, the term *hiilla(h)* is used to address other women friends and signifies a close friendship or kinship. There are few formal organizations for Crow women, but through activities, friendships among women are born and solidified. For example, women will say to other women, "*Hiilla(h)*—let's go get water." "Come and let us sew." "Come and let us play games [Indian women's dice game]." "Let us go to the dance." "Sit with me at the hand-game." "Let us pick berries." "Let us dry meat." "Let us go swimming." "Let us go sing with the singers together." All of these activities would exclude males.

Among men, organizations, societies, and clubs were more formal and became "friendship organizations." A friend *(iilapaache)* was one who shared experiences and activities. Some would live in each other's home for extended periods. Very close friends would continue to stay with one another even after marriage, treating the friend's wife as a sister-in-law. Others who could be called friends were fellow war-party members; men who shared the same woman, even as in the case of taking a woman during "wife-taking" activities; and members of formal clubs and societies, the most demanding form of friendship.

TELLING OF ONE'S ACCOMPLISHMENTS AND DEEDS—BRAGGING

It is unbecoming of a Crow to brag. To recount one's deeds outside of permissible situations is tantamount to bragging and hence frowned upon. When Crows tell of their accomplishments in an inappropriate manner, they are quickly reminded, "You are comparing yourself to me. You are saying your deeds are better than mine. I will take one of your prized possessions!" When there is occasion to tell of personal accomplishments and deeds, it is public and so announced. Retelling is in dramatic and emphatic terms. For example, it can follow an honor situation, such as the singing of one's honor song in a public gathering or dance. At the end of the song, the honoree will preface the retelling of deeds with "*Huuk a he! Hook a hay!* Beat the drums!" The staccato drumbeat that follows alerts listeners that worthy and outstanding deeds are about to be told. Oftentimes, the drumbeat signals that the accounts to be retold are so outstanding that few, if any, have ever repeated them.

If a group is rejoicing, as in a victory celebration, one can be selected to recount deeds for the entire group. In "The Story of Spotted Horse," there is a hand-game between two clan teams, and one person is selected to retell his deeds for the winning side. He prefaces his incomparable stories with *"Huuk a he!"* each time, signaling that each is a singular and dramatic occasion.

Not only is bragging unbecoming, but it gives the individual too much credit, as Crows believe that outstanding deeds and accomplishments are brought by Patron Spirits, a Greater Power, a Greater Grace, the Great Maker—God. Whatever one's occupation—warrior, athlete, hunter—it is only through mystical means that he or she is outstanding on the occasion of the event to be retold. Because of Crows' humility about their accomplishments, non-Indians and non-Crows are frequently confused and disappointed when interviewing individual Crows about their lives. Because they are obtained improperly, such interviews are "laid back," and the interviewees may appear to be timid and nondramatic. These interviews ultimately create confusion and distortion.

MARKING SACRED AND SOLEMN MOMENTS

The Crows punctuate significant occasions with symbolic objects and rituals. A pipe is offered to mourners, for example, to demonstrate the solemnity of the moment. There is no beating of drums. Deeds are recounted to highlight truth and the nonfrivolity of the occasion. In the sacred tobacco ceremony, a warrior is selected to recount his deeds prior to lighting the fire in the sacred lodge.

When sundancers pierce themselves, they can terminate the fasting and suffering only if the tether rope or the pierced skin breaks. To aid the suffering sundancers, warrior friends retell war deeds, announcing, "So that this was true, so now I will free my friend!" With that, they fling the suspended dancers to jerk them free. If the rope or the skin breaks, there will be a loud cheer and the sundancer is freed. But if neither the rope nor the skin breaks and the sundancer remains confined, there are often mumblings to express surprise and disappointment, disappointment that the story was not true because the sundancer was not freed, reflecting directly on the storyteller.

THE IMPORTANCE OF NAMES

Names of tribal members can be changed to reflect personal deeds. Names are also changed to bring better fortune, health, and long life, and the Crows believe that an untrue name will bring ill fortune. When adverse conditions such as illness prevail, names are frequently changed. No matter how pleasant sounding the name, it will not bring the desired results if it is not true. If this practice of truth in name giving is not followed, it is not the teller of deeds or name-giver who bears the penalty; it is the user or receiver of the name who suffers through ill fortune, poor health, and an undesirable life. When a name is bestowed, the bearer carries with him or her expectations of preserving that name's honor.

TERMINOLOGY IN THE TELLING OF DEEDS

The following phrases and characterizations may be found in accounts of Crows in battle and hostile situations. "Getting off" connotes getting off one's mount while in battle or being pursued. The gesture signifies that the warrior is standing his ground in bold defiance of the enemy. He is conveying the message, "I am just as good or better than any one of you!" This action was the measure of a real man. "Shooting down on" an enemy describes a sudden attack. When a warrior said, "I shot down on them," it meant that he attacked suddenly while the foe was still unprepared and unsuspecting, maybe even in bed. The term is also used to describe a shift of advantage. For example, one might say, "I finally overcame their resistance and shot down on them," indicating that the enemy was no longer in a commanding and defensible posture.

CLUB LIFE—SOCIETIES OF THE CROW

Crow clubs and societies were vehicles for friendships among men. Of the military societies, the major ones during the period immediately preceding the establishment of the reservation were the Foxes *(Iiaxxuke)* and Lumpwoods *(Balaxxishe)*. Membership in either of them marked the member throughout the tribe, often for life or in legend. Membership was subject to different circumstances, but the following were general rules.

Membership in the society followed the father's line. That is, if a man belonged to the Lumpwoods, then his son, his son's son, and every succeeding male of the father's lineage was pledged to that society or club. Paternal heredity was the primary rule for eligibility, loyalty, and membership, although actual membership was through an initiation ritual.

Men whose fathers were not members of a society could be brought into the club by friends who were members. A "friend" could be a close companion; a friend of a lost sibling; one from a different family or group who had performed or received favors; or one who had shared experiences, such as fasts, rituals, or battles.

Outstanding warriors had the mobility and flexibility to choose to which society they wanted to belong. The Crows tell and retell a story about two warriors who belonged to rival groups, one to the Foxes and the other to the Lumpwoods. The rival societies systematically claimed to have better men. Each group maintained that its members were better warriors, stronger, and otherwise superior to members of the other society. The rivalry was so intense that members of one group aspired to "take a woman" belonging to the other group.

A brave Lumpwood had taken the wife of an outstanding Fox during the spring club activity and "wife taking." Not long thereafter, there was a furious battle with the enemy, and there was little or no regard about who belonged to which club—everyone was a Crow and fighting the enemy as such. In the heat of the battle, a Crow warrior was surrounded. It was the Fox who had had his wife taken by the Lumpwoods. His situation was extremely hazardous and appeared hopeless.

A member of the Crow war party rode his horse into the thickest of the melee, fought off the enemy, and rescued the Fox by riding double with him on his horse. It was the Lumpwood who had taken the Fox's wife. Later, when the spring club activity was again in full swing and the rival clubs were looking for new and outstanding members, the Lumpwood rode into the midst of the circle of Foxes. He addressed the Fox whose wife he had taken and whom he had rescued in battle by riding double with him. "*Biilapxeekat* [one I have shared a woman with], I have come for you. Come with me to my club." The Fox responded, "So it is." With that, he jumped behind the Lumpwood on his horse and rode double, back to the Lumpwood circle. As they were riding away, the Lumpwood called back to the Foxes, "That is the way I got him back [rescued him]. If you want him back, get him back as I did [rescue him in battle], and you can have him."

This account illustrates one circumstance under which members of one society can change to another. The story makes clear that it was not done frivolously, but in an extraordinary fashion. The Fox and Lumpwood were friends first, Crows above all else, and they shared an experience that few, if any, had shared.

Leaders of the tribe depended on the societies because the outstanding members shared police action for the tribe. Chiefs and leaders would say, "On this day, the Lumpwoods [or Foxes] will be the police of the caravan." The club would thus be charged with the security, safety, and discipline of the caravan as it moved from one camp to another. Sometimes on these occasions, club members would pretend to be old women, even dressing as such. They were skilled warriors, but they were conveying the message, "I am like an old woman. I cannot run or try to escape danger. I will not run, but face the consequences." "Being an old woman" was not restricted to a moving camp or any particular situation. It could be done at any time, but always with the message, "I will not run [in the face of the enemy]."

CRAZY DOGS

Crazy Dogs were members of an exclusive club who vowed to die at the hands of the enemy. A Crazy Dog pledged to face the enemy in a most hazardous situation, in which life was exposed to the ultimate threat, and to face the fighting fearlessly and without retreat, to die in the process if that was to be. If he lived through it, he had completed his vow. Once surviving that vow, he was not bound to do it repeatedly until he was killed.

A Crazy Dog's vow might have come into play during a confrontation between the Crows and an enemy when there was a standoff, with neither side gaining an advantage. If word came that there was a standoff, the Crazy Dog seized the moment. He would fearlessly plunge into the enemy's fortifications and take as many with him as he could, trying to tip the balance in favor of the Crows. While the enemy was occupied with this fearless one, the other Crows would follow him into the fray, breaching the enemy's defenses. Such was the usual strategy and function of the Crazy Dog. He would be a legend thereafter, whether or not he lived.

There are many accounts of Crazy Dogs who became so endeared to the tribe that their deaths were mourned by many beyond their families and loved ones. Accounts recall that even married women openly mourned their passing and carried on in the traditional demeanor of Crows who had lost loved ones. Before members fulfilled their vow, they were afforded every courtesy and privilege. So extensive was the outpouring of feeling for Crazy Dogs that even married women shared their beds without re-crimination. Every favor to a Crazy Dog was considered proper because death was imminent; the special treatment paralleled the "last requests" of a condemned man. Crazy Dogs took liberties that others did not even dream of, because they were going to die.

Several phrases were commonly used to describe Crazy Dogs:

They "talked backward." That is, if Crazy Dogs were asked to do some-thing, they responded by doing the opposite. They were given to venturing through the camp in the company of a good singer (and drummer), looking for an invitation to pause and dance. If a Crazy Dog were told, "Stop here, pause, and dance," he would not stop and dance but continue on. Conversely, if he were told, "Do not stop here. Do not dance here," he would dismount, his singer would sing, and he would dance. If he were told, "Do not get off here and do not come in and eat," he would say, "So be it, I will not do so," then proceed to get off, come in, and eat. This kind of behavior grew out of emotional and psychological necessity. Crazy Dogs were conditioning themselves for the moment when they would face certain death and loved ones would plead with them not to go.

They dressed in red and wore long sashes that they let drag. Crazy Dogs wore the color of blood to show their disdain for the loss of it. The sashes also had a purpose. While Crazy Dogs were promenading or dancing, other men and women could pick up the sash and follow, as being led by the Crazy Dog. For men, this was a public signal that they would follow him into the battle and death march. For women, it signaled that they would have a relationship with the Crazy Dog, whatever the consequences. When others picked up the sash and followed, they were said to *iiaxcheeteek* (they hung on to his tether).

They liked to dance. Crazy Dogs would go through the camp, pausing now and then to dance. Their dance was unique and had a hypnotic effect on those who watched. Their dress and makeup were usually the ultimate in attractiveness, and they were the handsomest of men, made even more so by the knowledge that they were not going to live long. It was a last look at a living and breathing, handsome young man. A Crazy Dog carried only a gourd (rattle) and dressed in his finest, with the red shirt, leggings, and sash.

Crazy Dogs were given to serenading. They serenaded the camp at any time, particularly during the quiet of the night when the camp went to bed and sounds carried far and easily. Their songs were laced with lyrics that told of their will to die, the effect of their death, and other reminders that they had pledged to die. The following are lyrics of songs that Crazy Dogs sang:

> I am anxious to go [die]
> I am losing sleep because of [it]
> I will cause some of these [rascals'] wives to mourn and weep
> I will die, that is why I am doing that
> When you met me the last time [last summer],
> it made me lonely forever after [because I will be gone soon].

In all the things that Crazy Dogs did pending their moment, they meticulously and openly tried to crowd a normal lifetime's experiences into a very, very short time. This was the demeanor and lifestyle of a Crazy Dog once he took the pledge. The Crows have many stories of Crazy Dogs, and each is dramatic to the extreme. Of all the Crazy Dogs, one's story is told and retold, the story of Rabbit Child, which is presented here.

The Storytellers

This collection of stories has been translated from Crow into English by the brothers Henry Old Coyote and Barney Old Coyote Jr., both native Crow speakers. The stories themselves are put together from many renditions that were told to the authors at separate interviews.

PLAIN FEATHER

The primary storyteller for "Rabbit Child: A Crazy Dog of the Crows," "The Saga of Red Bear," and "Elusive Fame and Glory: The Story of Spotted Horse" was Plain Feather, a descendent of Top of the Mountain. Plain Feather's father was the brother-in-law to whom Top of the Mountain or Hunts to Die refers in his story of Red Bear's preparation for a victorious homecoming. The stories are told eyewitness style, as Plain Feather told them as he had heard them told and retold by his father and his uncle.

A respected storyteller, a tribal historian, and an outstanding singer of the Crows, Plain Feather was born around 1866 near Absarokee, Montana. The son of Hunts the White Calf II (father) and Comes Out of the Ground (mother), Plain Feather was also the nephew of Hunts to Die, who is central to some of the stories that follow and to whom Plain Feather attributed his knowledge of many stories. He was also the adopted son of Plenty Coups, a noted chief and respected leader of the Crow people. A child during the Battle of the Little Big Horn, he lived through the changing lifestyles of the Crows. In 1891, he married Lives High in Joliet, Montana, and built a house near Pryor, Montana, in 1906. For the bulk of his life, Plain Feather farmed and ranched on the Crow reservation just outside Pryor. He also hauled water for construction workers and animals while the Pryor

Railroad was being constructed, and served as a reservation policeman for many years.

Plain Feather played an essential role in the survival of Crow traditions and stories. He lived through a tumultuous time, witnessing the way of life that existed on the plains when he was a child transform into the reservation life that he knew as an old man. His contributions to this book are great, as he provided many details and songs in his renditions of the stories. He died on 24 December 1966, estimated to have been at least one hundred years old.

COLD WIND

Born to the Hidatsas near Fort Mandan (North Dakota Territory) in the early 1840s, Cold Wind spent the latter part of his youth and the rest of his life among the Crows, where he was a member of the Big Lodge clan. He spent much of his life as a scout for the U.S. Army. He began his career in 1878, when he joined the army and served in the Nez Perce campaign, wherein the army sought to prevent Chief Joseph from fleeing to Canada. A year later he served in the Bannock campaign in Idaho, afterward joining the B Troop U.S. Scouts at Fort Custer and patrolling the Crow reservation. He is known to be one of the first police officers of the reservation. Later, he was assigned to the L Troop, First Cavalry as a regular trooper, serving as corporal until 1895. From that time until World War I, Cold Wind worked as a farmhand around the reservation, briefly retiring from U.S. service. In 1914, General "Black Jack" Pershing requested Cold Wind join him in Mexico as he pursued the bandit Pancho Villa. Cold Wind had served under Pershing with the Black Tenth Cavalry, when Pershing was a lieutenant at Fort Assiniboine (near present-day Havre, Montana). He remained in Mexico with Pershing until the campaign ended and Pershing was sent to France to fight the Kaiser and Cold Wind returned to the Crow reservation. His descendents are proud of the fact that they have continued to be members of law enforcement.

Cold Wind was widely respected and known as a storyteller who could relate stories of the tribe before and after the split of the Crow people from the Hidatsas. He was a noted expert in the retelling of warrior stories, all the way back to the creation stories of the Crows. Placed in the Veterans Hospital at Fort Mackenzie, Wyoming, after going blind, he died on 22

January 1944 at 103 years old. He is buried at the Little Big Horn Battlefield on the Crow Reservation.

Cold Wind was a young boy when the men that these stories center around were progressing in age. While some of the accomplishments that are recorded in these stories had already taken place at the time of his birth, Cold Wind provided many details of events in these stories from his own memories. He was of a generation that still had a living connection with these men and their families, and he served as a window into the Great Plains era.

CARL CROOKED ARM

The narrative shifts in "The Years Following the Red Lodge," because the primary storyteller was Carl Crooked Arm, a grandson of Iron Fork, who was a contemporary of Top of the Mountain, or Hunts to Die.

The son of Crooked Arm (father) and Strikes That Catches (mother), Carl Crooked Arm was born in the Black Lodge District of the Crow Reservation in 1890. He was one of the early students of the tribe to attend the Carlisle Indian School established by Major Pratt at Carlisle Barracks in Carlisle, Pennsylvania. Known as an outstanding athlete at the Carlisle Indian School, he was called "the swiftest of the Crows" on the reservation for his racing abilities both as an individual and as a member of relay teams. Carl Crooked Arm was also known for his skillful tellings of Crow stories in the Crow and English languages, supplemented by songs and terms from the Lakotas, Crows, and other tribes. In 1911, he married Philomena Five and moved to Saint Xavier, Montana, where he farmed until his death on 7 August 1966.

Several other people contributed versions of the stories that supplement the primary storytellers' voices; they include Foolish Man, Old Coyote, and Mae Take Gun Childs.

23

PART 2

The Stories

Rabbit Child: A Crazy Dog of the Crows

It was a particularly severe winter in Crow Country. The snow was so deep and the weather so cold and severe that deer following each other would become bogged down in the snow. As the deer followed each other, the leaders would become stuck in the snow, and as others caught up, others would pile into the leaders and the deer would try to break new trails and become stuck in the snow and freeze to death. Such a time was referred to as "when deer fell" [*uuxe xape*]. Frozen carcasses were everywhere in the deep and frozen snow. Crow hunters went about searching for the fatter carcasses and brought the meat home, the larders having been depleted during the heavy weather, since hunting was difficult and game hard to find.

Rabbit Child had been wounded at the battle where White Horse's younger brother had been killed. The battle was "on the other side" [Big Horn Basin], and Rabbit Child had taken an arrow through the knee. Though the leg was strong after the wound healed, the ligaments had become stiff and he could not bend the knee. The leg was stiff. As his family and children needed food, Rabbit Child ventured out to where the frozen deer were, and he became more and more frustrated. Since he could not bend his knee, he could not negotiate the deep snow although plentiful meat could be had in the frozen drifts.

He said, "I am not old yet, but there will be many times when I am pitiful. I can only see years and years of frustration because of my condition. Rather than face that, I will die. I will die as if it meant nothing." This simple expression was known to an increasing circle of friends and relatives among the River Crows. It was Rabbit Child's Crazy Dog vow.

It was spring again in Crow Country and everything was good. Food was plentiful, the weather was comfortable, horses were regaining their fat, and spirits were high among the Crows. The main camp [Mountain Crows] was camped at *Iiaxupash* [just east of present-day Livingston, Montana] under the leadership of White Temple and his father, Sits in the Middle. It seemed as if the camp grew larger by the day as new groups and families arrived to add lodges to the already formidable camp along the Yellowstone River.

Everywhere in the open ground between lodges and the government buildings of the Crow Agency,[1] between the camps and the river and all the way to the foothills, it was springtime and joyful activity was found everywhere. There were horse races on the flats, kick-ball contests here and there, and the ever-present arrow games, as families, friends, and groups renewed acquaintances and passed the day with traditional activity of every description. Elderly men sat in large semicircles and the pipe lighters would light two pipes at a time, passing them to both ends of the semicircle. It was a time to reflect and renew spirits before the camp would break up and lead off in different directions of Crow Country for the summer. Young women wore beaded blankets to which were attached little bells that tinkled as they went about strutting in their neat, legginged moccasins. Good sights and good feelings were everywhere. Young men rode their finest horses and as they went from group to group, it was evident that they were anxious to capture the gaze and attention of the many young women wandering about. Everywhere one looked there was happiness and good things. The many lodges seemed to be equal in size and uniform for as far as the eye could see, from around the government agency grounds all the way down the Elk River [Yellowstone River].

From the lower reaches of the camp could be heard the unmistakable call of a Crow man wanting attention [a "war whoop" in present-day terms]. As the call echoed through the groups, people stopped to listen, each wondering who and what it could be at this most propitious time. Some were already saying, "It is probably Rabbit Child."

Rabbit Child and his horse were magnificent as he rode into view. The horse had belonged to Big Forehead [the hero of Rainy Buttes[2]], and it never seemed to lose fat, but always was in good condition. Crows had not noticed how well built and pretty the blaze-faced animal was until now. Good training and good conditioning were evident as this fine animal pranced and acted up under the sure hands of Rabbit Child. It was apparent to all that this was the prettiest horse that could be found in all the Crows' collection of fine horses. Over the back of this fine animal, he had thrown a half-black, half-red blanket, using a cougar hide for a saddle blanket. He attached a single martingale, with a colorful bridle and a bundle of myriad feathers on the forehead of the animal. These bounced colorfully as the horse threw its head up and down in lively anticipation of things to come. He was "rarin' to go." Rabbit Child was equally magnificent astride this beautifully adorned animal. He wore leggings beaded from hip to bottom and was resplendent in the colorful red trappings of the Crazy Dog. He pompadoured his foretop rather short and tied a full eagle tail on top of his head as a single ornament. In one hand, he carried a rattle with eagle feathers tied as ornaments on the top (it was a tin can, meticulously cleaned and scrubbed until it shone brightly in the sun). In the other, he held a rawhide rattle with a beaded strap, which he wrapped around his wrist. His long red sash drug tauntingly behind as he made his way magnificently into full view. The sash was wrapped around his torso both ways, bandolier style.

The magnificent horse and his rider were beyond description. What a sight! He striped his face with bright red paint, and dressed as he was, none of the spectators had ever realized how handsome Rabbit Child was until now as he rode into their midst, his rattle seeming to be too slow as he kept time to his deliberate song. Neither was it known that he had possessed such a beautiful singing voice; it was so smooth and even that it was almost hypnotic.

The blaze-face was even more magnificent as it would jump awhile in place, then jump sideways, seeming to lope in place, then again switch its hind legs to the other side and repeat the loping in place. After going forward a distance, the horse would sometimes stop, plant its feet, seeming to stretch its back and neigh in rich and bellowing tones. As this eye-catching pair made their way, it was as if the rider had told his horse, "I will just be singing as I ride you. You go ahead and put on an act as I sing astride you." His song was almost sad and lamenting as the melody and lyrics pervaded the now-hushed spectators.

> You young women,
> I have come,
> come outside.

Even women who had never known him could not meet his gaze, as

29

woman after woman found herself staring at the ground as his song and words seemed to pierce the very thoughts of everyone. He punctuated the end of his song with the loud and piercing whoops of a committed warrior. Then he began his second song, which was a bit more lively, but just as enchanting and haunting.

I am looking for a fortification [where the enemy is embattled].
I will go to enter it.[3]

There was trilling from countless throats of women, as the shrill and high-pitched notes blended in with praise songs from any number of proud men.

There were few, if any dry eyes as one looked about, as Rabbit Child seemed to hold his head even higher, even appearing to be looking up at an unseen scene above. As Rabbit Child was passing where the horse races were, one of the men stepped forward and called to him.

"Rabbit Child. Do not stop [pause] here. Do not dismount. Do not dance here, but continue on your way." Rabbit Child replied, "So it will be. I will not pause here. I will not dismount. I will not dance." Whereupon, he dismounted and, removing the hand drum he had kept slung over his shoulder, handed it to the men. The word went out quickly: "Find a singer for him." Singers for Crazy Dogs were very special, as the songs, drumbeat, and style were unique only to their dance, unlike other songs and rhythms. Some of the men disappeared into the camp while Rabbit Child demonstrated his extremely pleasing personality while they waited. He was very good natured, with a personality that endeared him immediately. He was quick to laugh, and there was always that infectious smile that exhibited his even and white teeth with the pleasant and handsome face. Soon the men returned with a tall, dark-brown complexioned man. His name was One with a Shirt, and he was known to have a clear, loud voice, much in demand as a singer in the tribe. It was One with a Shirt [a Whistle Water] who now spoke.

"Listen to me, you Crows. You ask me to sing at different things, and I oblige although the occasion may not be so good. This time, this is one of the greatest things in our respective lifetimes. I will be at his side. I will drum for him and I will sing for him [to the end]." With that, he broke into the rollicking, catchy chant of the Crazy Dog, complete with drumroll.

People ran on foot, on horseback, and from every direction as the clear song and unmistakable drumbeat permeated throughout the area. Never before had there been so many to witness a single person dancing as now crowded to see Rabbit Child. He was magnificent beyond imagination as he majestically performed the jumping-in-place step of the Crazy Dog, accompanying the rhythm with the smooth staccato rattling of his gourd. He was such a good dancer. Since he was going to die, he had no inhibition. He was dancing so gracefully, but so hard, that it was clear that Rabbit Child was totally committed to his vow. As he seemed to smoothly strain ever harder, he could occasionally be heard to say, "*Hih! Hih!*" He was good. He was handsome, and the spectators could not take their eyes off of his spirited dance. It was intoxicating to watch this handsome young man perform this dance that is done only by self-condemned men of the tribe. It was a mixture of fascinated admiration and haunting visions of viewing a man dancing his last moments on earth! It ended abruptly with little fanfare. The crowd had just witnessed the affirmation of a Crazy Dog vow, a vow to die!

The next day, the ritual was repeated. This time there was an extremely long procession that followed the Crazy Dog as he made his way to about the same place as the day before. Here again, he dismounted and his singer/drummer rendered the unique series of Crazy Dog songs. As he danced, more and more people crowded to view this handsome and magnificent young man. Just when the dancing and singing was becoming ever more spirited, Rabbit Child unsheathed a short rifle the Crows called "One with a Hump on the Handle" and loaded it in plain sight of the spectators. As he pointed the muzzle toward his foot, Rabbit Child said: "Just in case I might have a tendency to become weak of heart [resolve], I will give it a try [test my resolve]." With that, he blew a hole through his foot. As blood bubbled from the wound and his moccasin, he continued to dance as if he felt no pain, completely oblivious to the injured foot and the gasps that ran throughout the crowd.

Following Rabbit Child's promenades, dances, and serenades at *Iiax-upash*, his announcement to be a Crazy Dog and to die were on the lips of Crow people everywhere. The word traveled fast from camp to camp, from band to band until it seemed that all that the Crows talked about was Rabbit.

It was now early summer in the valleys and foothills of the Rocky

Mountains. Swollen rivers had subsided somewhat and the upper gullies were drying here and there. Animals were fat and newly hatched birds of every description gave testimony that summer was here. The camp at *Iiaxupash* dwindled ever smaller by the day as family after family, group after group broke camp to leisurely venture into favorite summering camps of the Crows. A large group (the largest of the groups) under the leadership of Long Horse [Long Elk] started its summer trek toward Belt Mountain and the Highwood Mountains. They would surely encounter Piegan and Gros Ventre [Atsina] during the summer.

Another large group of perhaps forty to fifty lodges, this one under the leadership of White Temple and other chiefs, was the camp that moved with Rabbit Child, the Crazy Dog. Because of his presence, many skilled and renowned warriors chose to stay with this group as it moved downstream, following the Elk River [Yellowstone River].

As the camp was preparing to move from *Iiaxupash,* a white trader at the government agency compound became disturbed and extremely excited, running from the Indian agency to the camp and back to the Crow Agency. The trader had not been paid for materials that Rabbit Child had taken, and now the camp was moving. When word that "Rabbit Child will die" reached the trader's ears, he became obsessed with the task of getting paid for goods and materials that Rabbit had not paid for but had taken. All the red cloth, the jewelry (rings, necklaces, broaches), and other adornment that Rabbit had used had come from the trader's store. The ruckus he created was unheard of to the Crows who fully understood what had happened. What was wrong with this white man who would dare to demand payment for things that a Crazy Dog had taken? Finally, White Temple and other leaders went to the trader and explained: A Crazy Dog enjoys unprecedented privileges once he takes the vow to die. He is given every courtesy and privilege by everyone. Even husbands would not fuss if the Crazy Dog would come to his lodge and say, "Let me be with her for awhile; you will have all her time later." Every one in the camp is given to making the last days of the Crazy Dog as pleasant as possible while he is alive. He is going to die and he has only a short time to live, so let him have everything he wants for nothing!

The trader refused to abide by these rules even after it was explained by the camp leaders and by White Temple. The chiefs then piled furs and pelts for the trader until he was satisfied that he had been adequately reimbursed for what Rabbit had taken. The camp moved in the direction of the Sioux and Cheyenne, toward the Big Horn River and foothills of the Big Horn Mountains. At each camp, Rabbit would do his inimitable promenading, serenading, and occasional dance. His dance was so eye catching and intriguing that it never grew old. Men from other camps even searched out the White Temple camp just to witness his routine, which was now the talk of all the Crows. His ready and spontaneous laughter would haunt his survivors later, but now as the camp moved ever eastward, Rabbit was the epitome of the Crazy Dog waiting for his day and his moment.

He would pause at any number of campfires in the evenings, telling stories in his catchy and unique style, bringing good feelings and spirits wherever he ventured. Still, he was as handsome as ever, and feelings for him grew ever stronger as he repeated his routine day by day, dancing now and then.

Screech Owl was a handsome young man. His name had not been too well known, although it seemed that everyone knew about him and that he was a fine young man. Now as the camp moved ever closer to the enemy, Screech Owl surprised everyone by joining Rabbit as a Crazy Dog. Screech Owl was equally resplendent in his red Crazy Dog garb, mounted on a very handsome horse known to the Crows as "the little gray," famous for his speed, endurance, and beautiful horseflesh. The camp was obsessed with one Crazy Dog, and now there were two. It was difficult to distinguish which was the more handsome, the better dancer, or which one tugged at the heart strings more. They were a sight to behold as they sometimes rode double through the camp or mounted singly and abreast around the fringes of the camp, singing serenade songs:

> I am looking for a fortification.
> I will go to enter it.

More and more came from other camps and bands to witness these two in these, their legendary last days.

Rabbit (sometimes with Owl and sometimes without him) continued his routine. He would stop where children would be playing and dismount, would clean them up, comb their hair, put perfume on them, and go to the next group of children. If children seemed unhappy or slightly injured, he would stop and comfort them, binding scraped knees and otherwise extending every kindness to defenseless ones. If he was enjoying a particularly good meal, he would save portions for the aged, saying, "Here, Grandmother (or Grandfather), I was enjoying some good food and I saved some for you." His manner and demeanor were everything that was to be expected of a Crazy Dog.

The two would even call groups of children to groom them, put paint on their faces, and showed kindness to an extreme. At night, they would serenade through camp, enjoying company with young women from all over the camp, married or not. Sometimes, they would even venture into lodges and say, "You will spend a lot of time with her. Leave and I will spend a moment with her," whereupon husbands would leave without recrimination, then or later. These were the short lives of Screech Owl and Rabbit Child. It could have gone on forever.

The camp was situated along Fly Creek where there are yellow sandstone outcroppings and where occasional cottonwood groves are frequently obscured. [This is a reference to present-day Fly Creek where it is crossed by the paved highway. It is called "where the entire camp mourned and wailed," a reference to the homecoming of the ill-fated war party and debacle at the Battle of Rainy Buttes. The camp was situated to take advantage of the occasional shade of the cottonwoods, and there were long, level stretches of open ground to the rolling hills on either side of the deeply cut course of Fly Creek as it meanders north, first from one side of the valley, then to the other.] Suddenly, from the south and west came the ever-familiar cry [war whoop] announcing: "Get on the alert, there are enemies near! Rise to the occasion, you rascals! There are some people [men] riding toward the creek with their war bonnets glaring prominently in the sun!" There was chaos, confusion, and activity everywhere in the camp. The enemy was near! Quicker than it takes to tell it, there were clouds of dust streaking toward the distant hills as warriors mounted their warhorses and whipped them to the attack. The enemy was not yet seen, but there was no doubt that a battle was at hand.

Some elder men gathered on one of the many prominent points into the valley, atop a cut bank. From there, they awaited some sign or word from the warriors who had disappeared over the divide. From that vantage point they smoked the ever-present pipe and mused over what might be going on over the hills. The sun was getting high in the sky and still there was no word or sight of the pursuing Crow warriors. Neither did the Crazy Dogs show any particular activity as the waiting continued.

Then a group of mounted Crow warriors abruptly appeared over the divide close to the creek and rode hard into camp. It was The Bull who was in the lead. He brandished some torn cloth in his outstretched hand. "You rascals, stay where you are. They [the enemy] were running toward the creek when I caught up to them and crowded this one [the enemy] and ripped off his shirt. I struck first coup!"

Runs through the Camp had taken a bullet in the knee, and blood was spurting over earlier bleeding from the wound. This was the awaited signal. Everywhere in the camp, warriors mounted their horses and raced to attack the enemy. Toward the hills, clouds of dust were streaking behind the many warriors who were now whipping their horses ever faster over the divide to the battle beyond. The enemy had taken a stand; there surely would be a fight. Even as the dust was just settling over the divide where the warriors disappeared again, the Crazy Dogs' song could be heard clearly. Their voices were loud and clear as the sound of their slow, heart-rending and haunting melody carried from the edges of the camp.

> Here and now,
> there is nothing that will make me
> live long.

They punctuated the end of the song with the piercing war cry of the totally committed warrior. They reached one extreme of the camp, and as they ended their song, they turned their beautiful mounts around and reversed their course in a slow and deliberate lope. Those in the camp wanted to turn their eyes away from the indescribable sight, but no one could take his eyes off of this handsome pair performing their ritual. As Rabbit Child and Screech Owl again skirted the very edges of the row of lodges in a slow gallop, their voices carried even clearer and farther throughout the camp.

> I am looking for a fortification.
> I will go to enter it.

They simultaneously punctuated the song with piercing and earnest war cries as they reined their mounts into a brisk gallop in the direction where earlier the warriors had gone. To tear-filled eyes in and around the edges of the camp, they were two red blobs, seeming to come together now and then and separating again as they swiftly made their way across the sagebrush flats to the divide. Then, they were gone from sight.

The enemy had made its stand along a dry stretch of the creek bed, protected by high-cut banks ringed with tall grass. The banks were high and a man could stand upright and still not be exposed to the surrounding Crow warriors. The crazy meander of the stream course made it impossible to approach the embattled Sioux in one group. They were up and down the creek in protected bends of the creek. From this cover, they swept the flats in front of their breast works [fortification] with withering gunfire. Even those on either side on the high ground were obliged to fire on them occasionally from behind protecting ridges.

Crow after Crow would make a run at the embattled enemy across the level ground on both sides, only to be driven back time and again, sometimes with wounded mounts. The battle rose and fell in intensity as no words were exchanged between the beleaguered Sioux and their attackers; there was only gunfire. Carriers of "Straight Sticks and Crooked Sticks" [society badges of warriors who vowed to stand their ground] ventured forth, and some symbolically swung their sticks over the cut bank, thereby completing their responsibility. At least one such stick was wrenched from a Crow.

Sporadic fire from Crow scattered throughout the sagebrush, and clumps of greasewood kept the enemy pinned down as much as from the sharpshooters along the high ground. Among those on the ridge overlooking the besieged Sioux were some of the most skilled and renowned warriors of the tribe. Pitted Face, Piegan, Warrior, and other famous warriors were keeping the pressure on the embattled Sioux.

Again, the unmistakable cry [war whoop] of a warrior calling for attention ranged through the battleground. "It is the Crazy Dogs. They have come." They were galloping as they disappeared from sight when they crossed a meander, reappearing on the nearer side, seeming to be two totally red objects alternately coming together and separating again as they made their way through tall sage and greasewood. Where the air had been filled with dust, blue smoke, and gunfire before, there seemed to be a strange silence now as all eyes of the Crows were fixed on Rabbit and Owl. The Crazy Dogs had arrived! They had tied their horses in the creek bed, and now as they approached along a depression, Rabbit Child was limping slightly (his foot not completely healed from his self-inflicted wound at *Iiaxupash*) and holding his rifle by the end of the muzzle. One of the Crows was the first to speak to the Crazy Dog. "Your friends [Sioux] are embattled in the creek bed. We fire on them but we cannot seem to move them out or do anything with them." It was Rabbit Child who responded, Screech Owl being content to let his partner do the talking. "That is good. There were times when we thought we would not see it this summer, but it is here. It is good." He laced his words with easy laughter and was grinning contentedly all the while.

"To the Great Maker, I give thanks. I was pleading that if there were an enemy, to please let me be there. It is good. If this carried on into winter, it would not be good. Thank you, Great Maker, for letting it happen now." Both Crazy Dogs were talking to each other as they surveyed the scene as it was being described to them.

"All right, Biilapxeekaat [one I share a woman with], let us look in there and find the spot that is the strongest and the most intense, for it will not be good if we enter their fence [barrier] where there is no resistance. Let us find the likeliest spot. So it will be. Let us go." Where before it had been a "no-man's land," the two ventured forth and peered into the channel, drawing some fire, but they had a good look. They came back and it was Rabbit Child who spoke.

"There is a real good concentration just downstream, and another just upstream. They are about equal; we can go to either spot. They are good. All right, we will go now. Look after yourselves. We will draw their fire [attract their bullets]; you can follow us at your will. Do not hesitate. If your bullets find us, that is fine. It makes no difference today if it is your bullets or theirs. We go now."

Rabbit Child loaded the short, stubby rifle, placed the butt on his hip and, fingering the cocked trigger, braced himself and walked deliberately and directly at the heaviest concentration of the embattled Sioux. Slightly to his left, but abreast, Screech Owl also braced himself and readied himself, as did his partner. The two seemed to be oblivious to what was at hand and even appeared to countenance a broadening smile as the air was shattered by angry gunfire.

"*Poom-poo-poo-poom! Poom-poo-poo-poom!*" Gun smoke belched from everywhere in front of the two Crazy Dogs and momentarily obscured the two red-clad figures. Rabbit Child did not stagger. His feet were planted firmly as his lifeless body crashed heavily to the very ground he had walked on but a moment before. He had fallen on his back, and a few steps to his left, Screech Owl fell heavily backward as more than a half dozen bullets smashed into him. Both had felt nothing, being dead before they hit the ground. All the gunfire from the Sioux came at an angle from below. A single bullet had shattered the butt of Rabbit Child's rifle, entered his torso at an upward angle, and stilled his strong heart. All the wounds in Screech Owl would have been fatal even if taken one at a time.

The Crows, who were witnessing this once-in-a-lifetime scene, sprang to the attack, swarming over the embattled Sioux who had no time to reload their weapons. Those on the higher ground rose up, and there were many targets now as friend and foe were all over the creek bed and on the banks. In a few violent moments it was all over. The Sioux were wiped out to a man. First coup had been struck by The Bull earlier. Many weapons were taken, as mop-up was not long to complete. But there was no singing and no rejoicing. The bodies of the two Crazy Dogs were removed, and sobbing warriors quietly piled rocks as high as they could reach to mark where the two had fallen. The monuments remain to this day.

It is told that Rabbit Child's mother would lead his horse and follow the caravan as it moved from one camp to another. When the camp settled, she would tether the blaze-face on a high hill overlooking the camp and wail into the night. She could be heard every waking moment because the body of her son was wrapped in a green buffalo hide and draped over his tethered horse. Young women, even married ones, would join her in her mournful vigil. She continued this until the leaders implored her to end her sad mourning because it was not good to keep the body so long.

The Saga of Red Bear

The story of Red Bear *(Daxbitche Hishish)* and his revenge is a classic in that it recounts the rise to greatness of one of the Crow people's outstanding leaders. It occurred within the living memory of retelling, occurring in the early 1800s, placing the story within the historical time frame, although with time, it is likely to become a legend. The essence of the revenge is an account by one of the actual participants, Top of the Mountain *(Awaxaam Aakeelash)*, later known as Hunts to Die *(Alasheechiilish)* and Longs to Die. In Crow he was known as *Shee-she* and was himself a legend.

Top of the Mountain was a nephew (or little brother) of the Great One, Red Bear. Red Bear was a man of great power, possessing mystical and supernatural abilities. He was a warrior of renown. His considerable reputation stemmed from his powers bestowed through the patron spirit of the Bull Buffalo. He performed many miraculous achievements with this power and medicine. His particular forte had been in doctoring wounded and otherwise unhealthy members of the tribe. He was a figure to behold and to fear. He commanded faith and confidence. He was kind and a protector, but his wrath and vengeance were fierce.

Although Red Bear's reputation and accomplishments with the buffalo medicine were well known, his recent visitation (during a fast and meditation, commonly called a vision quest) by the spirit of the Morning Star (Daytime Star, Star of the Dawn, and Star That Is on High are all terms identifying this significant heavenly body) had presaged a reputation even more awesome than before. His newly acquired powers and mysticism were subjects of constant and considerable speculation by members of the tribe, but one thing was certain. Red Bear was a giant among the Crows.

39

RED BEAR'S CHALLENGE

The Crow camp was at what is now the confluence of Mission Creek with the Yellowstone River, south of present-day Livingston *[Iiaxupash]*, Montana. The immensity of the camp made it appear that the uniquely white lodges of the Crows occupied the entire valley. This was a camp of the Mountain Crows, the main camp. Spring was here. The ice was gone from most rivers and waterways. The landscape was streaked and spotted with patches of hard-packed snow and persisting drifts along with persistent patches of ice on still waters. Even small drainages were swollen with muddy and snow-cold waters. Treacherous mud holes and soggy areas were everywhere. It was a time for replenishing depleted larders and parfleche storage bags. Change was everywhere. This was a time for new life, as this was the beginning of the most beautiful of all seasons, springtime.

But in the Crow camp there was no happiness, no uplifting of mind and spirit. Hearts were heavy and there was heavy gloom and despair through-out the camp. The Red Lodge band, which had been camping along the banks of the "Fast Current" *[Biliiliikashee* and *Ashhishalahaawiio]* some two hundred miles away, near present-day Red Lodge, Montana, had been wiped out. Thirty lodges had been devastated and ravaged by the Shoshones *[Bikkaashe]*. There were no survivors, no evidence of fate of family, friends, and relatives. All that remained were the devastated lodges of the camp chief, who had a red lodge, and that of his brother, who had a yellow lodge. They had been surprised and barbarously wiped out by a band of Shoshones. It seemed that most of the camp on the Yellowstone this springtime was in mourning. Those not immediately affected by the debacle at "Where the Red Lodge Was Wiped Out" were heavy of heart and sullen out of respect and sympathy for those who suffered the loss of loved ones.

Sadness and grieving seemed to be everywhere, but the desire for re-venge overwhelmed and even exceeded the grieving. To the mourners and grievers, there was a foremost and persistent thought: "Wreak vengeance and suffering upon those who are responsible for the devastation of the Red Lodge."

Others wished terrible and humiliating demise for the leader of those who ravaged the Red Lodge camp. Root-digging tools *[batchipe]* were everywhere. These were picks, three to four feet long with sharp points with which to dig roots and to use as tools of convenience. When in mourning, women would paint black stripes on the digging tool to signify the seasons during which they would remain in mourning for lost loved ones. One stripe would mean that the bearer would mourn for one season. Two stripes for two seasons and continuing until four stripes meant four seasons of mourning, or one year. It was in the midst of this that the "pipe was offered" to Red Bear. The offering of the pipe is not to be refused by any mortal. By accepting the pipe, the acceptor is then committed to the pleadings and petition of those who offer it. So significant is this practice among Plains Indians that "smoking the pipe together" heralded the total absence of malice and animosity. Warfare and even battles would be curtailed and set aside when the pipe was offered. If the pipe were held out, those fighting would not violate the sacred pipe, but would be obliged to sit down and cease all hostility. Similarly, when the pipe is offered among friends, it is to preface a request, which is not to be denied. When you are offered the pipe, and you accept, you are then bound to adhere to whatever it is that is asked of you. In some instances, entire tribes and bands would offer the pipe to other tribes and bands, thereby mobilizing an alliance to jointly pursue whatever endeavor might be at hand. In the Pryor Creek Battle, where the combined forces of the Sioux, Arapaho, and Cheyenne gathered to "wipe out all the Crows from the face of this earth," it was said that these tribes "offered the pipe to each other." This indicates that the three tribes had gathered all the forces they could to accomplish the task of wiping out the Crows.

In this case, the offer to Red Bear was not just the pipe. It was accompanied by gifts of all description. He was offered all those things that are desired and cherished by men of the tribe. Included in the offering was a beautiful young maiden, just reaching young womanhood and a virgin; she was beautiful, clean, of good family and reputation, and desired by all men who would lay eyes upon her. This raven-haired beauty was legend even during her declining years on the Crow Reservation where she lived out the last of her years at Pryor, Montana. Her name was Woman on Earth [*Awaakeenbiash*], and this beauty was Red Bear's to have as his own if he would only accept the challenge. The challenge was to wreak revenge upon the Shoshones for beating the Crows so badly at "Where the Red Lodge Was Wiped Out."

Implicit in this challenge was the desire of the tribe to gain particular revenge upon the leader and perpetrator of the carnage of the Red Lodge. Old women in short-cropped hair and stubs for fingers; young women with short-cut hair, wearing only black; men, young and old, with their hair cropped short and tens and tens of people carrying root-digging tools [grieving sticks]; these along with mourners who unashamedly bore open festering wounds all peered intently upon the imposing figure of Red Bear as he surveyed the offerings and contemplated the sacred pipe that was now offered him. [The scene was intense and grim because Crow people in mourning would disfigure themselves by cutting off their fingers and cutting themselves and leaving open and festering wounds—all commensurate with the degree of grieving. A standard badge of mourning was the cutting off of long hair, long hair being a measure of attractiveness. Mourning was a period of wearing black and generally being unkempt and unattractive.]

Would this great man be up to the revenge, which was in the hearts of all these wretched beings seeking that revenge? Would revenge finally be theirs? Were the offerings enough to consider in the light of the expectations, which surely are on the minds of all who are here to witness this offering? Would he personally accept the pipe and hence accept the challenge? Or would he accept it only to pass it on to another? That was after all permissible because the offer of the pipe would not be violated if he would accept it conditionally. By passing it on to someone else, he could gracefully bow away from the challenge without violating the discipline of the pipe.

"*So it is . . . already [Kootaahisht]*"! With this, Red Bear majestically but humbly took the pipe. There was no cheering. No rejoicing, no dancing, no singing. There was only the quiet relief of knowing that a major step had been taken. There would be "another day," and hopefully soon.

The entire camp went to bed, went to bed wondering when the Great Man would rise and seek out the Shoshones who so mercilessly ravaged the Red Lodge. It was shortly thereafter that Red Bear came to Top of the Mountain [Awaxaam]. He was not yet known as Hunts to Die [Alasheechi-ilish], and his name meant "One Who Is on Top of the Mountain."

"Little Brother, I want you to come with me," Red Bear told him. "I will have things for you to do. You will help me. You know what I am to do and the time is here." Top of the Mountain had been a helper and scout for Red Bear on a number of previous war parties of which his uncle was the war-party chief. He had served him well on those occasions. Top of the Mountain had no equal when it came to the war-party trail and serving as a scout. He was fleet of foot and long on endurance. He could run all day. Red Bear prepared for the mission and imminent war party in accordance with age-old practices of the Crows. He and his assistants, his supporters, and others who wanted to visibly venture on the warpath with him ran through camp. This was the announcement: they were embarking on the long-awaited mission to avenge "Where the Red Lodge Was Wiped Out."

Red Bear's verbal announcement was simple and to the point: "I will travel across the foothills of the mountains toward the land of the Shoshones." He said, "You may join me if you wish until the fourth night."

Crow war parties would leave the camp; usually in the dark of night so as to keep their total members secret. Individuals could join or leave the party with no recrimination until the fourth night, when there would be war-party tales and feasting, and pledges and desires were revealed. No one was allowed to leave or join the war party after the fourth night until the enemy was sighted.

THE WAR PARTY

As the war party proceeded along the foothills of the mountains, individuals and groups caught up with it and joined. The war party, under the sure and deliberate leadership of Red Bear, proceeded with no particular haste. The numbers grew and grew until there must have been at least two hundred or more bodies. There were some on horses, but for the most part this was a "pedestrian war party," traveling on foot with the sure knowledge that they would return mounted on the good horses of the Shoshones, horses that were renowned for their beauty and solid horseflesh.

Everywhere one looked there were the ever-present root-digging tools. The mourning sticks were carried for the purpose noted herein, but there was now another purpose: the stick would be "cleansed" by striking the enemy with it or piercing his flesh with it. Once this was done, the mourning was finished. Vengeance would be accomplished.

It seemed that there was an unusual number of women in the war party, all clutching root diggers! In the vanguard of this great procession marched Red Bear. He was even more imposing than when he was still in the camp on the Yellowstone River. At his side, carrying his shield and other personal

43

effects, was the beautiful Woman on Earth. Her every movement reflected the grace and beauty that was uniquely hers on this, her first war party. It was a magnificent sight. It tended to wipe from the mind, at least for the moment, the great grieving that had given rise to this war party.

Top of the Mountain maintained a respectful distance from Red Bear. This was the customary demeanor of one who harbors and displays respect for a Great One. The Great One was afforded a distance, aloofness, as a sign of the respect that was commanded by his mere presence. Top of the Mountain maintained this distance although he had been asked to come by Red Bear himself. Top of the Mountain marched along, as did the others, reflecting on the great challenge that they all now shared: to gain revenge for the Red Lodge.

Top of the Mountain also had a woman along. He had taken her from her husband. Top of the Mountain was a member of the Lumpwoods, and she was a wife of the Foxes, her husband being a member of the Foxes, a rival military society. [This practice has been called "wife stealing," but the term does not describe the practice completely. It was "taking of another's wife" and reflected that the husband was not truly worthy of the woman or that the woman was not the sole property of the man. The theft was to the everlasting prestige of the wife-taker, while for a woman, running off with another man suggested that he was a better man—much to the shame and disgrace of the loser.

There were several warrior societies, with the Foxes and Lumpwoods as principal rivals. Rivalry centered on prestige and having the best men of the tribe. One would make every effort to outdo members of the other society, even in battle or on the warpath. A measure of this was the taking of the rival society's wives.]

So now, Top of the Mountain had with him the wife of one of his rivals. Having her did not end the matter. In essence, he was saying, "Poor woman. She has no honor being your wife. With me, there will be honor and prestige and I will demonstrate that she could have a better man!"

He turned to look at her once again. She was not too tall and somewhat on the portly side, not bad looking, although not the beauty who was carrying Red Bear's shield. She seemed to be unmindful of the thoughts that were racing through Top of the Mountain's mind, but appeared to be content to be with her new husband and in this war party. Both wished that there would be no regrets and shame when they returned. If this turned into an empty trip, they would both be scorned by friend and foe alike. Their respective reputations would be ruined, hers for lacking character and being unworthy of her first husband. Members of the Foxes would forever look upon her with disdain, not admiration or respect. He would be ridiculed for daring to take a woman with much promise and not being able to fulfill those promises. Both would be without honor.

These thoughts were racing through Top of the Mountain's brain as he wondered what role and tasks the Great One had in mind for him. One thing was certain. This war party had to be a success, for there was too much riding on it. Finally, they arrived at the edge of the Big Horn Basin in what is now the sagebrush country of northern Wyoming where the Clark's Fork River flows north as it comes out of the great mountains. This was a country well known to the Crows and was referred to as "On the other side"—the other side of the Big Horns. Everywhere there were barren hillsides, as there was no vegetation on the shale and bentonite outcroppings on the rolling and undulating hills.

Red Bear's scouts had done their job well, Top of the Mountain being one of them. They had selected a campsite that was well protected from the elements and not conspicuous to the searching eyes of the enemy. Sentries had good vantage points from which to survey the surrounding countryside without being conspicuous themselves. The campsite afforded every advantage to regroup, reorganize, and prepare for the formidable task ahead. The scouts had good fortune hunting. Meat was plentiful. There were the fat-laced choice cuts of fat buffalo cows and the succulent meat of elk that had wintered well on the nourishing salt grasses. The bounty of the scouts' hunting included tender morsels from unwary deer that dotted the trail and had been easy pickings.

In the midst of all this, the war party made camp. There being no other wood or brush with which to construct the wickiup lodges of the war party on the trail, the warriors, even the women, set about constructing wickiups with the sagebrush that was everywhere.[1] They were as big as trees, and comfortable lodges quickly appeared for the major expanse of the large coulee bottom where the camp was established. The gently sloping bowl provided a campground that was probably the best under the circumstances. There were over a hundred lodges, some housing as many as four and five people. Top of the Mountain and his woman shared a lodge with Red Bear and his beautiful bride of a few days. Their lodge was not too large, but it was comfortable when they stored their gear and sat down to feast upon the tasty meat. Sage-wood fires burned and the pungent-sweet smell of burning sage was everywhere. Meat cooking on spits and burning fat generated an aroma that permeated the length and breadth of the camp, awakening appetites that had been steadily growing with every step of the journey. The smell of good food was everywhere and again the spirits dared to pick up. As night began to show its first signs and the old, old man Sun wrapped his scarlet robe around himself and was disappearing from sight, one of the "real he-men" of the war party ventured forth to talk loudly enough so that most of the camp could hear him. Only real he-men who had demonstrated their bravery and prowess spoke loudly on the war-party trail. It was one thing to make public pronouncements in the safety and comfort of one's own home camp, but on the war-party trail, these were privileges only the proven ones could take. Speaking with the authority of one who had done this time and again, he said, "Red Bear, the time is here. Whatever it is that you are going to do, do it now. Begin; the time is never going to be any better."

With that, Red Bear issued final instructions to go with those directions that had been given from time to time since the war party left the Yellowstone. "Prepare the Lodge. Prepare the floor and door. Get things ready. Prepare food and we will eat when I finish. I will begin now!"

The lodge was quickly cleared of extraneous gear and trappings. The floor was scraped free of grass and other plants. The ground was shaved clean. The floor was then again swept and made ready after spreading cushions for seats all around the periphery of the inside. The entryway was closed and the fire was made to burn down until only a few embers cast a dim light upon the ring of faces in the lodge. No one was permitted to walk upon the floor after it had been swept. The articles that were taken from Red Bear's medicine bundle would now rest upon an unfettered and clean Mother Earth with nothing in between. Red Bear's patron spirit was the Morning Star, giving him untold powers that had not been open to scrutiny by members of the tribe. Living persons had never before seen his ritual and ceremony. All eyes in the lodge were on this Great Man who would now reveal things to come and how he would meet the challenge that he accepted on the banks of the Yellowstone.

Even those outside the lodge waited with bated breath for the slightest sound to come from within the lodge. The sentries at the entryway did

1. Barney Old Coyote Jr., 1970

2. Barney Old Coyote Jr. (*left*) and Henry Old Coyote (*right*) at the Crow Fair, Crow Agency, 1940

3. Barney Old Coyote Jr. (*left*) and Henry Old Coyote (*right*) Lawson Field, Georgia, 1942

4. (*Above*) Patricia Old Coyote
Bauerle, 1970

5. (*Above right*) Alanna Kathleen
Brown, 2000

6. (*Right*) Phenocia Bauerle, 1997

7. Plain Feather, 1920s–1930s.
Courtesy of Hardin Photo

8. Cold Wind, ca. 1920s–1930s.
Courtesy of Hardin Photo

not need to bark instructions; everyone knew what was at hand. Top of the Mountain sat just to the right of the Great One. Red Bear's upper torso was painted solidly in yellow. There was a large star emblazoned in red squarely in the middle of his chest. There were two smaller stars similarly in red on each shoulder, facing forward. His hair was placed in a considerable bun on top of his head and laced with metal balls that shone, seemingly too brightly, in the dim light. His entire face was painted a solid yellow and ringed with a bright red border. His torso was similarly ringed with bright red paint. Around his neck hung a huge [eagle] wing-bone whistle, painted yellow. The whistle, etched in green with the zigzag pattern of the lightning symbol, hung from a section of otter hide. The paint combination gave a strange concave effect to his face and gave him an eerie and foreboding appearance, truly a breathing image of the spirit of the Morning Star! He burned incense upon the smoldering embers, and as the sweet smell permeated the lodge, Red Bear began to sing. His chant was a rollicking and enchanting melody, the lyrics brief and simple:

> When [where] I go . . .
> I will go well [it will be good].
> I go to eat! [Eating or devouring also meant the defeat of the enemy.]

He paused, as if waiting to hear something. The silence within and outside the lodge was total. One hardly dared to breathe. A glance at Red Bear clearly showed that if he was not in a trance, then surely he was not with us on this plane; he was somewhere else. He sang the stanza and lyrics only once and became reflective. We knew that he was not addressing anyone in that lodge, certainly not the mere mortals who hung on every word of his song. It was a strange and enchanting melody that would haunt those who were listening to it, who would later find themselves humming it absentmindedly.

As he momentarily paused and meditated, he appeared to see something more clearly. What it was we did not know and did not pretend to know. His voice was full of confidence and authority and he broke into another song, only this time the chant was more somber and solemn, as if a great burden were now at hand. This new melody and rhythm was not too unlike a Gregorian chant. His rich, deep voice rose until the hair on the back of our necks seemed to stand straight up and chills raced up and down our backs. The air was electric as he repeated the lyrics, which again were simple and brief.

What I saw [in a vision], will be!

With that he finished his song with a call similar to that used by camp announcers. The series of sounds that carry the message: Pay heed. Pay attention. Be responsive. It will be so!

His prominent chin rested on his formidable chest, and he let his head drop, as if to signal that it was done. There were no praise songs, as is customary. The weight of the mission was too great.

He said, "Light the fire. Let there be light. Tomorrow we move. It is done." With that signal, "fire starters" were thrown upon the dying embers. [These were wads of dry, paper-thin tree bark that had been rubbed soft and saturated with fat and grease. When they were thrown on the embers, they would flare and the fire would be restarted in immediate light and flame.] As they flamed up now, there was a brightness in the lodge and one could feel the sighs of release, even outside of the lodge, where unintelligible babble replaced the overwhelming quiet that had been there but a moment ago.

After Red Bear shed himself of his ceremonial garb, feasting was everywhere. Although Top of the Mountain did not fall off to sleep right away, there was well deserved and contented sleep throughout the night that was laced with the sporadic sounds of the nocturnal. The new dawn approached. Soon the Morning Star would come in all its glory.

Red Bear publicly called Top of the Mountain to his side: "Top of the Mountain, you go from here with whoever will go with you. Go in the direction of 'Fringe's Father' [present-day Thermopolis, Wyoming], where Fringe had fasted and was visited by the spirit of the Big Spring of Hot Water. It had been called his Father, Patron Spirit, as a lasting landmark to this day. There is a 'saddle' on the horizon as you look toward Fringe's Father. Aim for that. You will go to the lee of that prominent point that juts into the basin away from the mountains. There you will see a high point with a conspicuous monument of rocks on top. Just to the side of that hill there is a small coulee that drains into a larger coulee. At that point, there is a fallen tree that points its top to the south. Right there along the trail lies a dark-willow quirt [whip], covered with blood with the wrist strap broken. When you find that quirt (the strap wore through and the owner does not even know it broke off), look to the side of the obvious trail. Under a piece of tree bark there is a twist of tobacco lying on the ground. It belonged to the enemy. The tobacco has had some water on it and the twist is warped and peeling. He put it there, then forgot it. Bring that tobacco and I will smoke it.

"I will move with the camp to just this side of the lesser point, where there is a large expanse of level ground on top of that plateaulike shelf. I will camp there and wait for you. You go and find what I told you. Once you have done that, you perform the ceremonial return of the scout *Batchikaaku(h)!* [The term *Batchikaaku* has been used through the ages to proclaim the confirmation of the nearness of the enemy—to know that he is within reach and that a battle is imminent.]

Red Bear continued, "The distance is great. Go now and come to the camp and *Batchikaaku(h)* tomorrow!" He implored other young men to join Top of the Mountain. "Some go with him. You are many; don't let him go alone. Go with him, some of you!"

With that signal, Top of the Mountain looked about. Never did he feel so alone. Not a person in the vast throng showed any sign of wanting to join him now on this, the very first foray against the enemy. They were now venturing into the enemy's own ground to confirm the vision and prophecy of the war-party chief. He had proclaimed it with no doubt whatever! Top of the Mountain's routine was a familiar one as he prepared himself for the formidable and demanding task before him: to confirm and proclaim that the enemy was near, both in time and location. He had performed this routine many times before and had done it repeatedly with Red Bear. He tightened his moccasins around his ankles and bound the arches. They were high topped to protect the legs, and these he bound securely and firmly. He tied his large abalone-shell earrings with a string around the back of his neck, where they shone oddly out of place. He wore a dark-topped light shirt that he frequently wore when going out after horses and which was comfortable when he was moving fast. He rolled his Hudson's Bay short coat tightly and wound it around his waist along with a small quiver of arrows and his long spyglass.

After he had secured his apparel and equipment, he draped a wolf pelt, bandolier style, across his left shoulder, and secured it on his right hip. This was the traditional style of the Crow scout, and he was now fully equipped for the task at hand. He was streamlined and prepared to perform his specialty—the fleet, cunning scout who did not know the meaning of fatigue once on the trail! Scouts were like marathoners; they were fleet of foot with immeasurable endurance. Like the marathoner, their goal was predetermined and they accomplished the run in the shortest possible time.

Top of the Mountain's prowess as a scout was unequaled. He could run all day. He was as fleet as the driven snow and never was known to tire visibly, even momentarily. As he readied himself, it was obvious that he was geared for fast and furious movement, relying only upon his speed, cunning, and endurance to accomplish the tremendous task thrust upon him by his uncle. The Great One had said on the Yellowstone, "I will have things for you to do." That moment was here and he was all alone, so very alone, as he stood in plain view of all who witnessed this telling of Red Bear's vision and prophecy.

Red Bear said loudly, "It looks like that's it. It is just you. Go!" Top of the Mountain started out on a sprint when there was a call from the throng, "One is going with you!"

What a relief! Now he would not be alone. He turned to look and his gaze fell upon a handsome young man strutting forward. He was so handsome that he held your gaze as you first looked upon him. His foretop was almost shiny. His hair stood straight up from the forehead in the traditional style of the Crows [Indians call the man's pompadour "Nez Perce style"]. He was slim of waist and hips, with prominent thighs and calves. As Top of the Mountain looked him over, he mused to himself, "By all that is sacred, he will never last or keep up with me. I will leave him in no time."

The young man was Bear Who Approaches Downstream [*Daxbitche Buluakssaahush*], or Bear Approaches, widely known for his prowess as a bowman. He possessed considerable mystical powers, his medicine being the medicine arrows. This was good. Top of the Mountain would rely upon him for that specialty if there came a need.

All was ready. Top of the Mountain turned to Bear Approaches and asked, "How would you like to do this?"

Bear Approaches replied, "You do it in whatever way you do it. This day we will do things your way. Let's go!"

With that, they broke into a sprint and kept that pace all the time that they remained in sight of Red Bear and the war party. The coulees and draws were brimful with dark and foreboding waters. They even had the appearance of concealing underwater monsters ready to pounce on the unwary who would venture into the swirling depths. You could not look anywhere and surmise that there was a dry spot. Mud and water were everywhere. When there was an open stretch and footing was sure, Top of the Mountain would sprint and sprint, and as he let up his partner would come up on him, sounding like his breath was being knocked out of him, but blurting out, "Keep going, keep sprinting. Turn it on. We have far to go."

What a man! Never before had Top of the Mountain been pushed by another on the trail as he was now by Bear Approaches. Their backs were covered with mud and their shirts and short running leggings were beginning to hang heavy. All of a sudden, Bear Approaches caught up and said, "There it is. There is the peak with the monument. You have arrived."

The two unlikely companions had been running so hard and pressing so completely that they had lost all track of time and distance. They only knew the direction they kept and the need to press on ever harder. And now they were here. They slowed to a brisk walk and surveyed the surroundings. There was the large coulee, and sure enough there was the smaller coulee draining into the larger. Bear Approaches said, "Here is the fallen tree."

As they approached the tree, the trail became obvious and plain even to the untrained eye. To these two, it looked like the well-traveled path that it had been. Signs were easily read by the two expert scouts.

It was Top of the Mountain who found the quirt. It was blood caked, showing that the owner had packed meat on his horse. The wrist strap had broken and it was lying on the trail where it had fallen. The words of Red Bear were still ringing in their ears when Bear Approaches said, "Here it is. Here is the tobacco." It was lying under a piece of cottonwood bark just as the Great One had said. They put the tobacco in Top of the Mountain's shirt and wedged the quirt in Bear Approaches's belt. He was wearing essentially the same apparel and gear as his running mate. Irrefutable and physical evidence of the enemy's presence and of Red Bear's prophecy was now in their possession. They took one last look around before they took the long but more relaxed trek back to the main war-party camp, which lay waiting over the hills and across the many swollen gullies.

Bear Approaches said, "What is that pile of things over there?" Upon investigation, it was found to be meat from the hunt. It was piled neatly and marked with the saddle blanket of the hunter to claim when he returned for another pack load. They were in the midst of the enemy hunter's cache! "You rascal. Let's get out of here, out of sight and out of pursuit!"

They were in full flight. They had been running hard on their journey to the appointed spot. Now, they ran even faster. They ran so fast that it appeared that every evil being was breathing hot on their backs. Never had that country seen so fleet a pair as now vaulted sagebrush and hurdled rocks and brush. They ran and ran until it seemed that they had been running forever; still, neither could shake the other. As they topped over a ridge, Bear Approaches breathed it more than he muttered it: "There they are. There is the camp."

Before them, on the broad flat land on top of the plateau, was the camp with blue smoke pointing to the sky, seemingly from every lodge. Hunters were returning from the teeming herds that were everywhere, and they could see the people moving about the camp, busily but leisurely.

Both Bear Approaches and Top of the Mountain had carried their face paint and other accessories for just this occasion. They stopped and painted their faces as befitting one who "confirms the enemy" and readied themselves for the grand return. They moved closer to the camp and assumed a position where they were visible to the naked eye. Top of the Mountain spoke to Bear Approaches. "*Huummishi* [Do your thing]!" he said.

Bear Approaches was blessed with a loud and piercing voice. He later was a mainstay of the Tobacco Dance as a singer. He excelled in the scout's call. This was the call of the coyote, called the "birdcall of the coyote." It was a high-pitched falsetto and carried far beyond the range of the normal yell. Bear Approaches, after a moment of reflection, raised his face to the sky and gave forth with the shrill high notes of the call, descending to the more guttural and chesty conclusion.

Top of the Mountain was watching the camp through his spyglass. As the call ebbed lower in its echo, people in the camp paused from whatever they were doing. You could see them turn their heads, and some were even doing a series of quarter turns. They were turning their ears to the four winds, trying to catch some indication as to where the sound was coming from. "They hear you. Do it again!" Top of the Mountain told his partner.

They ran closer to the camp, where they could be seen. Bear Approaches found another vantage point and let loose another lingering call, this one seeming to be even more piercing and more shrill than the first series. Top of the Mountain looked again through the spyglass. Bedlam and turmoil were everywhere. Entire quarters of animals were dropped where the bounty of the hunt was being returned. Horses and people were in profusion. Men and women were dashing in and out of the lodges, and others were running to the edge of the camp to search for visible signs of Top of the Mountain and Bear Approaches. Their signal had been unmistakable. "The scouts have returned!"

Everyone had been waiting, and now the news spread like wildfire to envelop and possess the camp. The enemy was near. Things were readied for the "ceremonial return of the scouts." Buffalo chips were piled high at the edge of the camp. Members of the war party took their places, and the singers began singing even before the scouts were close. The group appeared even larger than it was as they held rank and position, leaving ample room for the scouts to approach the towering stack of buffalo chips. If the enemy was confirmed and the battle imminent, the two scouts would not need to speak a word. They would charge the pile of buffalo chips, trampling them underfoot. Upon this signal, the singing would pick up and the bystanders would dance through the buffalo chips, trampling them underfoot as they emulated the scouts. As they danced, the war-party members would take turns "counting coups on the scouts," with shouts of "*Haa-heh*" and striking the scouts as they would strike the enemy. They were dancing a fantasy of how they would count coup on the enemy. After all, these scouts had been there and back. There was no doubt. The scouts had been nearest the enemy.

When they were in plain sight of the camp, the two scouts broke for the camp in full sprint, jumping and hurdling sagebrush as they raced down the slope to the camp. Such swiftness, such speed! They were not unlike two young deer frolicking and chasing each other through the tall sage! Top of the Mountain did not press his hardest, and Bear Approaches kept pace, although slightly behind his running mate.

They paused, spun around, let out a yell, and crashed through the stack of buffalo chips. Sham battles and pantomimes broke out everywhere. Crowds systematically counted coup on the two, to the accompaniment of "*Haa-heh, haa-heh*." Red Bear asked, "Is it true?"

"*Yes, yes, yes!*" came the reply.

What a sight! What an event! The moment was near! There was rejoicing and high anticipation everywhere. It was midafternoon and feelings ran high throughout the afternoon. One particular sight remained in Top of the Mountain's memory for years.

One with a Mother was an unusually dark, heavy, portly man. His horse was a tall rangy buckskin with a long body. As he rode his horse in a walk, the horse appeared to be unusually flexible and would bend in the middle with each step. One with a Mother would appear to be dancing to an unheard tune as he kept the dance in a riding position. It was he who was singing a cheerful, rollicking song:

The lodges [people—the Shoshones] on the other side are giving me good things!
They are giving me a person [a boy].
Thanks forever and forever more because I will own one of their children . . .
These wretched and despicable beings dared to make me suffer and humiliate me.
Now it is my turn and I will take one of theirs home.
That is my mission.

These were the words of One with a Mother as he repeated the song over and over as he rode in and out of different areas of the camp. There were other and lasting memories throughout the camp, but the sight of One with a Mother riding his flexible horse, singing his song, and dancing from a riding position would remain with Top of the Mountain for the rest of his life.

The singing and rejoicing continued into the night. Top of the Mountain meanwhile returned to the lodge he would again share with the Great One and his bride. The food was good, and Top of the Mountain was tired, although he would be the last to admit it. Red Bear fixed his handsome and athletic nephew [little brother] with an uncharacteristic long stare. Top of the Mountain was beginning to feel somewhat uncomfortable and asked, "What is it?"

The Great One spoke: "Top of the Mountain!"

"*Heeh,*" Top of the Mountain responded.

"If I were you. If I were fast of foot and athletic as you are, and if you were me, sitting here with this woman in this lodge, I would not spend the night here tonight," Red Bear said. Top of the Mountain's woman was in another lodge with women friends.

"You do not want me here tonight, you want me to leave?" asked Top of the Mountain. He glanced at Red Bear's woman. She, too, fixed a steady gaze upon him. How big and beautiful her eyes! She continued her gaze.

It was Red Bear who broke the silence.

"Yes, I do not want you here tonight. I want you to leave. That is why I am saying this to you. Leave tonight and see day at that long ridge on the other side of where you found the quirt and twist of tobacco. Go downstream from there a bit. Go and see the covering of the lodges; they will be all white."

The announcement was made. "Top of the Mountain is leaving tonight to fix the location of the enemy camp in the morning. The rest of us will follow and meet him at a place predetermined by him and Red Bear. If you want to go with him, he is leaving now."

Whereas no one had stepped forward when he left for the first time and he felt so alone, there were now about thirty eager braves who waited in the pitch-black dark of this moonless night. It was with good spirits that the eager group left camp and disappeared into the night. The camp retired to what would be a short night before tomorrow, the day that would be "another day," all the way from the banks of the Yellowstone River!

There was not much in the way of skill among the group when it came to negotiating the many perils of a dark night in the midst of a muddy, messy runoff in the gumbo hills. Through the babble of people trying to lead others who were also trying to lead, one could hear exclamations: "Don't come this way; it's terrible! This is really deep and cold! I fell into a blind coulee!" These and other exclamations were heard with the grunting and straining as members of the party found themselves in the extreme darkness, trying to make some distance in unfamiliar surroundings, but happy nonetheless. Top of the Mountain and Bear Approaches assumed the lead and aimed for the tall and long ridges, which were now becoming visible. On they pressed. Dawn was just breaking and the Morning Star was in all its brilliance when Top of the Mountain announced, "We are here."

They set about changing their footwear and clothes. They were a mess, but breakfast was quick and welcome. As daylight began to bathe the countryside in its early spring brilliance and clarity, Top of the Mountain fixed his spyglass upon the not-too-distant stream and valley. He was just ending a sweep with the telescope when something white caught his eye. He returned the glass to that point and recognized not only one lodge, but an entire camp! He handed the glass to Bear Approaches, who also did the same sweep, and then everyone joined in the sighting. Down there on a stretch of slow and dead water in a protected and iced bend of the river were seventeen lodges, pitched on the far side along banks that were caving into the river here and there. The enemy had been sighted! His lodges were in plain sight! The scouts waited and some even napped, giving the main body time to come to where they could be seen.

Soon they came through the tall sagebrush with their weapons and digging tools prominently protruding above the tall sage as the war party wended its way to the rendezvous. As soon as the war party was even with them, the call of the scouts was made. The main body stood ready to receive them, and soon the "ceremonial return of the scouts" was again in full swing. This time there were thirty scouts who had seen the camp, but among them, all eyes were on Top of the Mountain. It was he who first "saw the lodge of the enemy," who had led both forays to confirm the presence of the enemy and who now briefed one and all on the "lay of the land." It was he that Red Bear relied upon and he had performed well. He was handsome to an extreme, and his woman of a few nights swelled with pride as everyone joined in the frenzy to make ready. "We are here and the enemy is here." "Today is the day." "Do your thing."

THE EDGE OF CAMP

With the enemy camp so near, the entire war party made ready. There was a flurry and bustle of activity as veteran warriors readied their weapons and donned battle paraphernalia. These usually were from medicine bundles that had had their worth demonstrated, while others would be tested for the first time. There were rookies facing their first battle who sought sponsors to bring them blessing and give them good fortune and opportunities for honor. Some would consummate previous arrangements with more powerful types so as not to go into battle "unprepared." They did not do anything for nothing; they had to have backup!

Among this war party against the hated Shoshones was a giant of a man, Spotted Horse *[Iichilixaxxish]*. He was a longtime champion of the Crows, a good man to have on your side and at your side. With his prowess and reputation, everyone in this war party, especially Red Bear, knew that it could well have been Spotted Horse who led this day. Now it was Red Bear who spoke loudly as to be heard by all in the party: "Spotted Horse, what is wrong? What is the matter? You are here and yet I have not heard from you. If it were you in my place and I in yours, I would surely have done something by now. Whatever it is, you have done nothing and you have been unnecessarily quiet! What is the matter? Why are you behaving so?"

Spotted Horse's voice was deep and rich, and his reply was one with complete control and authority: "All right, already. We did not occupy the same bed [meaning that when the two men fasted, it was in different locations, with different visitations, leading to different sources of supernatural powers]. There is no such thing as doing things exactly as others would do them. I will do it now, my way."

Spotted Horse had come prepared to do his part in wreaking vengeance on the hated Shoshones. Now Red Bear, the war-party chief, who was sure to be compared with Spotted Horse by all who were here, had thrust him into the limelight, and all attention now fell upon Spotted Horse.

"Pile buffalo chips right over there," Spotted Horse said as he pointed just to the east of where they were standing. "Pile them as high as you can reach, into a tower!"

Young and old, men and women quickly set about collecting buffalo chips, which were everywhere, and soon there was a towering mound of buffalo chips as high as a tall man could reach. Spotted Horse spoke as loudly as Red Bear before him. He began to peel his clothes off as he spoke. "You will see me stand on this pillar of buffalo chips. I will climb it! If so much as one or two fragments fall or I do not make it, I will return home from this very spot! You, Red Bear," he continued, "go ahead to yonder camp and have your fun, without me! Gain your honors by yourself!"

As he talked and shed his clothes, it was obvious that he had prepared himself well, for this, the most important day of those who were witnessing this giant of a man. He was a huge and angular man, and Top of the Mountain took in every detail as he watched Spotted Horse in awe. What a figure to behold! He had painted himself all in bright red paint. There were spiraling lines on each leg from ankle to knee. Hoof marks, as from horses, were painted from his knees, along his thighs, and up to his hips. He had similar spiraling lines from his wrists to elbows, then hoof marks along the biceps to the point of each shoulder. Countless sundance scars and gouges on his chest and abdomen were streaked with the same paint. [Sundance scars were from piercing the skin and tethering the sundancer

57

until the skin or rope broke. Gouges were U-shaped cuts, self-inflicted with a sharp tool as offerings.]

Spotted Horse's scars were so numerous that his entire front appeared as if he were wearing a breastplate painted in bright red clay! Sundance scars on his formidable shoulders and back were flecked in red, causing a profusion of red, rampant on his shoulder blades and back. His hair was piled high in a bun on top of his head. The bun was specked with lead. The abalone shell barrette at the back of his head was now tied on top, protruding forward. It contained some feathers, but magpie plumes were prominent as they pointed past his brow and eyes. He did not paint his face. This was the man they called Spotted Horse. As he stood there stripped of his clothing, his thick and broad ribs showed on his powerful sides. In each hand he carried matching wings of the eagle, and the yellow-painted wing-bone whistle hanging from his neck seemed so much larger than others that Top of the Mountain had remembered. Spotted Horse began to sing. The song had an ever-increasing crescendo, which suggested that it would surely lead to an ear-splitting climax.

> When I go searching for things,
> I will go right in front [right in the face],
> nothing will ever, can ever . . .

He tailed this off with the man's style of trilling into a higher and higher climax! The song punctuated with repeated shrill and loud whistles. He whistled again and again as if he were pressing for an even more climactic sight than we were watching. This imposing man walked about toward the base of the tower as he repeated the song again and again. Each time the song ended, he whistled and whistled. As he walked, he no longer walked like a man; he was strutting about as the great bird walks with bowed and postlike legs. By the fourth stanza, he was at the base; he whistled and whistled!

Just as Top of the Mountain blinked or took his eye away for a moment, there Spotted Horse was, standing in a crouch on top of the gigantic heap of buffalo chips. His stare was nonhuman as he gazed intently about with large, round eyes! Just as suddenly as he ascended, he turned and approached Red Bear. Where Spotted Horse's face had been unpainted before, it was now brightly painted in red around the entire periphery of his face! His ceremonial face paint had been applied by the very sun that shone brightly overhead. "There they are over there on the ice. There are ravaged bodies of the despicable ones [the enemy] scattered all over. I have one of their rifles, the wretched scums!"

As Spotted Horse finished with his ritual in preparation for the battle and of his own pronouncement prophesying what was to come, similar rituals were taking place all over the sagebrush flats leading to the camp. It was at this point that the announcement was made.

"Yonder camp is the enemy. There will be three coups to strike and count," proclaimed Red Bear. "First, there will be the usual, the striking of the enemy himself [first coup]; second, the one who strikes the lodge farthest upriver will count [another or second coup]; third, the one who strikes the lodge farthest downstream will count [another or third coup]. There will be three coups for this war party. Know that all of you!"

The strategy was set. The race for honors would be furious, there being three targets of opportunity. Not only would the enemy be ravaged, but the entire camp would be devastated, from the lodge farthest upstream to the last one downstream!

By now the war party had arrived at the river. The opposite bank was passable here and there, with ice all over, as this was a protected and shaded part of the river where it was leaving the mountains. Here and there gravel bars were in various stages of caving in along the riverbank.

"If you have not already opened your medicine, do it now!" voices in the party cried.

Again, there was a flurry of activity everywhere. Top of the Mountain's attention fell upon one of the rituals. This was Possessive Bear *[Daxbitche Baa Aaxxinesh]*. His medicine was the brown-tailed hawk. Plumes of the bird were tied on top of his head, and he wore a shirt with a dark blue top and blue stripes across the front. His young brother, who was going into his first battle, was similarly garbed and carried a long lance. Dressed as they were, Possessive Bear and his younger brother looked like identical twins. Possessive Bear held his brother by the shirt in the back and told him, "I will sing four times, then push you forward. You strike the red willows over there and say anything, or feel anything, anything you want to and it will be so!" With that he sang a somber and lingering tune.

You listen for things . . . try to hear things.

This part of the song was long. In a much shorter stanza he sang:

You listen to me, hear me!

Possessive Bear finished his song with a piercing yell and pushed his brother so hard that he stumbled forward and almost fell. As he rose, he hollered aloud, "I have one of their guns—the wretches!"

Another warrior deep in his own ritual was carrying stalks of sage, the kind with tiny round tips, so that he appeared to be holding little bells. As he smoked these over incense, he sang a lively and rollicking song. As he ended, he punctuated it with loud puffs—*Hih! Hih!* Yellow paint, with which he painted his face, was flying everywhere. "I will take their rifles!" He cried.

Top of the Mountain had now witnessed two singular events in which men with power had painted their bodies without laying a hand on themselves; they had been painted through a great power! Top of the Mountain did not have to look far to catch still another ritual in progress.

This was a man with eyes that tended to be squinty. The area between the nostrils and mouth protruded somewhat. His name was Fast Bear *[Daxbitche Xushish]*. He had a cap from the head of a grizzly, red in color. Feathers were here and there, with a down plume prominently floating about in the back. Small bells hung as in a fringe across the face opening.

Paint, the face is still proud.
Paint, the face is still to what I am singing,
Paint, the face is still . . .

So powerful was the melody of this ritual that it is one still used in the Crow Tobacco ceremony today. Fast Bear blew and red paint flew everywhere; he painted his cap with it.

Paint from unseen sources was held in high regard as being miraculous. And now, Top of the Mountain had just seen three such miracles. Top of the Mountain was waiting and nibbling some food with another uncle. The uncle said to him, "There is Red Bear over there. He brought you. Surely he did not bring you just because you are fleet of foot and long on endurance. You have served him well. Go to him. Tell him, 'Do something for me.' Then, if he does not respond, come back and I will paint your face. We want to take some of their guns."

As he approached, Red Bear was burning sweet grass for incense. He smoked the muzzle of his own rifle. You could detect the sweet smell from a distance. Red Bear was telling the others, "Do this, all of you. But do not bring any arrows to smoke." In spite of that admonition, some managed to smoke their arrows in the smoke. Some of the war party were wounded with arrows. As Red Bear was finishing smoking the rifles, Top of the Mountain called to him, "Red Bear!"

The Great One turned and said, "Come here." Why in the world did he not come earlier, this one, Red Bear thought to himself. "Come, come and get me that bundle right there behind me." Top of the Mountain picked up the considerable bundle and handed it to his uncle, his big brother.

"Wait. Wait a moment for me, every one." The Great One cleared a patch of ground. He untied and removed the bundle's contents. It was a long and broad otter skin decorated simply with the antler prong of a young bull elk. As he unceremoniously flung it on the cleared ground, Top of the Mountain saw a puff of dust fly up. Red Bear called to his nephew, "Come. Come and put your left hand in first and then your right." As he did so, Red Bear helped him put it on as one would wear a bandolier, with a strap over the left shoulder and the long part hanging on the right.

"Come. Come," Red Bear continued as he led him past a patch of gravel and made him stand in front of him. Red Bear pitched his face toward the Sun in the sky as he spoke.

"All right, Dear Father. This is the one called Top of the Mountain. Wherever [whenever] I go in any direction, he goes in front of me [as a scout]. He sees to it that I eat well. He makes sure that I sleep well and that I travel good trails. He guides me all over. He does all those things. This is the one. I was going to strike coup [first to strike], take his gun [the enemy], capture the sorrel paint, and have that woman [Woman on Earth] lead the victorious procession home. Father, not this time. Let it all be done by this one. This is the one called Top of the Mountain. He makes us eat and sleep well. Will you do it, Father?" Red Bear asked as he finished the blessing.

He turned to Top of the Mountain. "Go now. You will accomplish all three. He gave it to you. You will do it all. Now go and do it." Top of the

Mountain donned his Hudson's Bay jacket and mounted his roan horse that had just been broken to ride recently. The roan still wanted to buck and pitch when first mounted and spooked frequently. It was lively, the kind of horse a good rider wants under him. Those on foot led the way. They carried long sticks, and whenever anyone on horseback tried to pass, they would beat him back into the pack; they were strict monitors. They wanted to have an even break at getting at the enemy! Red Bear was right behind the pedestrians. They had gone but a short distance when he said, "Stop and pause for a moment." Everyone paused to hear the Great Man.

BATTLE—THE ENEMY IS OURS!

Word came from the front: "Top of the Mountain, Red Bear wants you to go to him." He did not need to kick his horse. He just eased up on the twist rope, and it appeared that the horse's back legs were yawing as Top of the Mountain made his way quickly to the Great One's side.

"Top of the Mountain, you go ahead around the bend and look things over downriver. Assess the lay of the land and how we might charge. Go now. Let him through, I am sending him."

The pedestrians let the horseman through. The roan was increasingly showing its anxiety, and his back legs yawed even more as he appeared to be skidding from side to side as Top of the Mountain made his way quickly out of sight of the war party. It was right there in front of him as he turned the knob of a knoll at the mouth of the depression he had just left. The lodge almost touched his horse's nose as he reined in and turned. He hurried back to the party, which was now almost upon the knob and the camp just beyond. His eyes immediately sought out Red Bear amidst the weapons, lances, and root-digging tools that covered the entire breadth of the depression. He started to say, "Just beyond that cottonwood . . ."

Red Bear's glare was piercing and his brow deeply furrowed with obvious disgust, if not outright and disappointing anger. He had sent his nephew ahead to strike coup first, but Top of the Mountain now returned without fulfilling what his uncle had so cleverly arranged. Red Bear knew that the enemy camp was just around the knoll ahead, and that sending Top of the Mountain literally assured that he would be in the camp ahead of anyone else, collecting all the honors with little or no competition. Red Bear had even breached the discipline of keeping horsemen behind the pedestrians, and now Top of the Mountain returned to the main pack empty handed with everyone growing more restless with each stop and breath. Red Bear's voice was like a red-hot prod.

"Top of the Mountain is no man after all. Why did he come back, anyway? I thought he was a man and wanted to accomplish manly things. What a nonman."

The realization of what he had done left Top of the Mountain numb and chilled. He felt nausea, but what was at hand was already obvious to this throng anxious for revenge. The ground shook and rumbled as the charge swept through the mouth of the depression! Top of the Mountain turned his mount around. It reared and made a jumping turn. He lashed him a couple of times around the rump and across the belly. He was in full and fearful charge! He did not remember that the first lodge upstream was a countable coup; he did not even think about it until he was a full three lodges into the camp. It was too late to turn back. He reined toward the river, as the camp in front of him appeared empty. The camp had been alerted to the approaching war party, and many had taken cover in the willows while still others were scrambling to make it across the ice and to the willows, the driftwood, and the cover beyond. The banks of the river on both sides were alive with people running and stumbling for cover. Efforts to meet the charge were unorganized and hurried!

Top of the Mountain rode right to the brink of the riverbank in a couple of places, only to find the bank too high. He saw one spot that had gravel and sand on the ice. It appeared to have been used as access over the ice. He gave his horse the rein. Man and horse were airborne as the roan vaulted off the bank. As hooves met the ice, all four feet went one way and Top of the Mountain another. They were both sliding on the ice as he clutched the roan's mane to keep his balance. They were still sliding on the ice when a husky Shoshone man bolted from cover and ran toward the sliding and struggling man and horse. He had a rifle in each hand. A glance made him to appear as if he had upright horns as he held the guns in front of him with the muzzles pointing upward. Top of the Mountain never took his eyes off of the Shoshone as he scrambled to his feet with the agility and quickness of the athlete that he was. The Shoshone came to a stop to level his guns. Then, both his feet flew in the air. He fell flat on his back as his head hit the ice with a sickening thud. One of his guns went clattering across the ice. Top of the Mountain picked it up and struck the Shoshone, with a "Haa-heh," with the Shoshone's own gun as Top of the Mountain jumped over him. He turned just in time to see the Shoshone bringing the muzzle of the other gun to bear upon his lithe figure. Top of the Mountain killed him on the spot.

Top of the Mountain looked up to whence he had come while the smoking gun still clouded his vision. The Crow charge had already enveloped several lodges, while others were being torn down and shaking everywhere in the upper section of the camp. In less time than it takes to tell it, *he had struck coup [daakshe ditchik]* as the first striker! *He had wrenched a gun from the enemy [ishadaxxia dutchik]!* And, he had been the first to dispense with the enemy.

As the charge surged through the Shoshone camp and across the ice, resistance was quickly quelled—so great was the intensity and fury of the charge! The men of the Shoshone camp had gone hunting early that morning, making the resistance much weaker. Now the war party ranged through the camp and back and forth across the ice. Everywhere there was gunfire, which seemed to rise and fall in intensity as new pockets of resistance were found and stilled.

From the lodge farthest upstream all the way to the last one downstream, the camp was being ravaged. Booty and burning lodges were everywhere. Booty was even on the ice among still and prone bodies of those who had not found cover. The willows were routed of those seeking cover. Captives were herded into groups isolated from one another. One could hear mixed cries for help and agony as Crow praise songs rose above the cries now and then. There was a tall, rangy Shoshone woman who ran from group to group. She caught Top of the Mountain's attention. She was looking for her child who had become separated from her during the charge and the ensuing but short-lived battle. She would come and repeatedly pound on the Crow men, then turn to plead with them in Shoshone. Of course, they did not understand. She kept running back and forth between the Shoshone and Crow groups in desperate search for her child.

Suddenly, around the bend downstream from what had been a stately camp came armed horsemen, riding hard. The war party had returned! They had sensed that things were not right at the camp and had cut the hunt short and returned to check. What they saw made the blood curdle. They beat their horses, and some did not even bother to change to their fast buffalo horses. They charged on whatever they were riding at the moment.

They were met by a fusillade of bullets and arrows. The battle was joined. Gunfire resumed and became even heavier than that which accompanied and sustained the Crow charge.

It looked for a moment that there would be a lengthy standoff as both sides probed and maneuvered. The tall Shoshone woman was seen pounding on some of the Shoshone men. She would eventually be among the captives that the Crows took.

Even as the area between the Crows and their enemy was repeatedly swept with gunfire and occasional volleys of arrows, out strode this tall (for a Shoshone) and powerful man. He spoke loudly and could be heard on both sides.

"Hear me, you Crows. I am Splintered End *[Uppiluussachish]*. There is no other. There is no other by that name. None among the Shoshones, none among the Crows. Just me. It is I who was at the 'Swift Current' where your relatives were killed. It is me that you want. Take me if you can."

With the words numbly falling on the ears of those who heard and understood, he packed his gun with sweet grass [appearing not to use bullets]. After so loading his gun he would fire with a yell, and the ricochet would sing and ring through the woods and over the ice. Crow after Crow jumped and tumbled for cover. Individual trees began to have more and more Crows seeking cover behind their trunks from this man who seemed immune to Crow weapons. Trees seemed to be not big enough. This was Splintered End, leader and chief of this band. He would drive a peg in the ground, picket himself to that peg, and walk around it as he made loud announcements and pronouncements. This was a sign that he would never run from his camp, no matter the peril! As he stood in plain sight in defiance of the Crow warriors and their weapons, it was clear that this was no ordinary foe. He had backup and he came to fight, to the end if need be!

The word went out quickly among the Crows: "Be careful. He might harm you, even by accident. Take care."

Crow sharpshooters carefully tried to bring down this hated destroyer of the Red Lodge. They fired without exposing themselves. Still he stood there, pinging shot after shot at the Crows, who now had doubts hovering in their minds. His yells continued to rise with each resounding shot. As the Crows burrowed deeper behind their cover and as they traded glances,

65

the word sped quickly up and down the breastworks: "Red Bear is going to shoot him!"

Red Bear's many blessings and talents included mystical power with the rifle and gunpowder, evidenced by the smoking of the muzzles before the battle. Red Bear now hurriedly performed his ritual, using the sweet-grass incense as before. No one saw him load bullets; witnesses only saw him load the sweet grass in his gun. He rose and all eyes of the Crows were on him. *"Poom"*—the report was deafening. Splintered End staggered backward and slowly fell to a sitting position. The missile had broken his leg just below the knee. Even from that distance, the Crows could imagine that they saw his stunned and incredulous face. Again the ice and ground rumbled.

Crows, men and women, broke from their cover. A large number of them charged the crippled and fallen leader. In a moment, the milling throng totally overwhelmed the spot where Splintered End had fallen. You could not see him from a distance. Severed limbs could be seen flying through the air as the throng decapitated and dismembered this hated enemy until only the truncated and limbless torso lay twisting and writhing on the ice!

Root-digging tools, some bloodstained, could be seen near the site of the carnage and throughout the battle area. At the same time, the Crow warriors charged the enemy ranks with renewed and frenzied fury. With their leader gone, the enemy's resistance was only token at best. Soon all was quiet on the ice and in the camp as stragglers were hunted down and dispensed without mercy.

Top of the Mountain hurried away from the ice after one quick look assured him that Splintered End was no more. He came to a plum and rosebush thicket where a number of horses were milling, away from the large herd that was now the scene of Crows scrambling to catch prized Shoshone horses, even women among them. As he was about to leave this milling band of horses of every description, he saw him. It was the sorrel paint! He expertly fashioned the end of the twist rope that he was using for a rein into a loop. He kicked the lively roan, forcing the sorrel paint against a heavier stand of the thicket, and looped the end of the rope around the paint's neck. It followed him easily, being a gentle and well-trained horse. *He had taken the sorrel paint in battle [ilichiin dutchik]!* Red Bear's third prophecy had now come true! He could hear gunfire in the distance now and then, but he could not wait to find Red Bear.

Red Bear had told him, "Do all those things, but keep the sorrel paint for me. I want the woman [Woman on Earth] to ride it when we ride victoriously through the camp."

No survivors were left in the camp. All able-bodied men were killed. Those surviving and able to travel were taken captive and brought back to Crow Country, such was the devastation and vengeance this day. Mop-up activities continued long into the day. There would be the battle to relive from the many accounts that were sure to be shared. Details would be sifted and deeds and other details confirmed and fixed under Red Bear's sure and strong leadership. For now, Top of the Mountain continued to look for Red Bear.

The war party straggled back to the mustering point of a few minutes previous. From every bend and thicket of the river bottom came herded horses and captives. Most of the captives were women and young children. From almost every Crow's back and every newly captured horse hung booty of every description and color. Not a Crow was afoot! Prized Shoshone horses were everywhere. Spirited yells and greetings pervaded this spring day across the dells and swales of the valley wall. Even as the straggling groups trailed back to where the packs and extra gear were stored, and even before they had regrouped and compared accounts, particular elements of the encounter were clear and on the lips and minds of all. Top of the Mountain had struck coup, captured a gun, and captured the sorrel paint. He was the hero, three times over.

Pretty Eagle *[Deeax Itchish]*[2] had struck the lodge farthest upstream, so he was the "second striker," having struck the camp first *[ashe koochik ditchik]*. Old Alligator *[Buliksaa Xaaliash]*[3] had struck the last lodge downstream, making him the "third striker," because he was the first to range through the camp and strike the very last lodge *[ash buluakussake ditchik]*.

The war party was an unqualified success. Enemy warriors had been routed and wiped out. The camp's residents were routed and taken captive to a person. Not a hoof of the Shoshone horse herd was left in the wake. The camp was mercilessly ravaged and laid to waste. A ball-like and limbless torso was left lying on the ice. Revenge was complete. The war party had met the enemy and revenge was theirs! With only a few arrow wounds, the Crows suffered no losses. Red Bear quietly went about the now familiar routine of regrouping his war party and prepared for the victorious journey back to the Crow camp. It was a routine Red Bear had performed many times before, but none with the satisfaction that now permeated throughout the totally successful war party.

The tall Shoshone woman walked deliberately and uncowed as she strode about the ring of captives. She would later escape, never to be seen by Crow eyes again. Top of the Mountain's woman followed the Shoshone woman's movements with lingering interest, then her eyes caught the steady gaze of Woman on Earth. The look they exchanged expressed it more eloquently than words' tearful satisfaction—joy and pride welled over!

AFTERMATH: THE RETURN

The lodges on the other side are giving me good things!
They are giving me a boy . . .
Thanks forever and forever more . . .
Because I now own one of their children!

As the joyful and lively tune rolled across the sagebrush flats, for all appearances it looked as if One with a Mother's buckskin horse was bending in the middle with every step. He bounced to the catchy tune, virtually dancing from his riding position. On his back, bouncing with him, was a young boy, tied around the buttocks with the strap slung over the dark, portly man's huge and rounded shoulders! It would be folly to guess what the young boy might be thinking as he surveyed this totally unfamiliar scene with drowsy-heavy eyes and lids! [Crows are prone and quick to distinguish other tribes by physical characteristics. The Shoshones are short, stocky and heavy, and unusually dark. Their hair, lashes, and brows are even blacker than the night. Their eyes are big and distinctive, appearing to be heavy to the point of sleepiness. The lids are heavy and the thick, heavy eyelashes appear to weight them down even more.]

All around there was happiness. The procession now strung out to twice the size of the party before the battle. Captives were everywhere, with a few choosing not to ride but to walk ignominiously as they were herded toward Crow Country. New mounts were being tried and tested everywhere as the dust and powder of the fragile landscape were kicked up into the sky, the rising dust visible even from a great distance. At the vanguard, the Great

One and Woman on Earth surveyed the great procession. What a sight! What rejoicing! What a great feeling!

They crossed the many divides and waterways and as they began to find themselves in the land where the sagebrush was as tall as trees, pulses quickened. Crow Country was near. Spirits were high everywhere. Societies were pulling rank on newer members; pranks thrust upon rookies by senior members evoked uninhibited and raucous laughter throughout the party.

"Gather the ropes to tie [lodge] poles." [This was the signal to begin preparing for camp just as the procession crossed the Sage Creek near what is now Frannie, Montana.]

Even the horse herders were made to walk until they were dog tired. As the appointed campsite came into view where the "child's footprints are" on the Clark's Fork River, the traditional homecoming songs of the victorious war party were now raised in all their glory. As the throng, mixed with captives, surged toward the campground, there was singing everywhere. Black paint was on faces everywhere you looked.[4]

There was no more grieving, no more sadness. There was only joy, rejoicing, and more of the same. The mourners who had pressed for revenge now had paint on their faces for the first time since the Red Lodge massacre. It seemed that their joy even exceeded the joy of the rest of this surging and happy crowd. No root-digging tools could be seen. They had been cleansed and discarded. Horses were everywhere although the horse herders had been made to walk today. There was no grief, no gloom. There was nothing but joy and high spirits.

The Lumpwoods and Foxes in the war party immediately organized their unique ceremonies of celebrating a victory. Members of the rival clubs appeared to want to outdo each other by calling members of the rival club by friendly names, in the spirit of fellowship of the occasion. Calls of one club member to members of the other club were frequently heard as the two rivals magnanimously greeted and treated everyone in sight: "Biilapxeekaat! One I share my woman with, my friend! Come share this food!"

It was during this club style of the victory celebration that Top of the Mountain formally took his woman, to have and to hold, through public pronouncement. During the victory celebration the Lumpwoods and Foxes took positions opposite each other to razz, ridicule, and perform acts of derision toward the rival club. Derisive songs, loud pronouncements, and other demeaning gestures were enthusiastically exchanged. A crowning blow was when the Lumpwoods flaunted one of the Foxes' wives in front of their faces—the woman that Top of the Mountain had taken. She was made to ride double with a fellow member of the Lumpwoods who was renowned for rescuing comrades in battle by riding double in the face of the enemy. He had singular and unquestionable right to ride double. Some Lumpwoods, with Top of the Mountain's woman riding double with him, then charged the ranks of Foxes, skirting their ranks while the other Lumpwoods loudly taunted them: "Look at that woman. She was your wife, but she knows who is good. She came on her own volition and free will." This was the public announcement.

As night fell, lodge poles sprang up all along the river bottom. For the first time since leaving the Elk River [Yellowstone River], all were in comfortable quarters. Even the captives were made comfortable while under heavy guard. Top of the Mountain did not share a lodge with the Great One this night. He was dog tired, and after the abnormal amount of food he had eaten, his woman gently stroked his head so as to put him to sleep. He could hear the animated babble of the day's events being told and retold and told again till he fell off to a deep, restful, and contented sleep.

The next morning after hunters had left the camp, his uncle sent for Top of the Mountain. When he arrived, he found Pretty Eagle and Old Alligator already at the Great One's side. The three heroes had been summoned, and now Red Bear spoke. "Your third member [Old Alligator] stepped on an elk horn and his foot is badly swollen. The two of you heroes go with Brave Bull to those hills and bluffs downstream and look for the camp. They may have moved downstream. Look for them and return quickly."

He gave Top of the Mountain a specially prepared shirt he had kept for just this occasion. The three mounted their fast horses and in no time were overlooking the confluence of the river. Top of the Mountain played his glass over the valley. Heavy, blue smoke hung like a giant cloud. Closer examination showed people all through the trees and brush. In the neighboring hills people were everywhere. Puffs of gun smoke could even be seen now and then as many hunters collected deer, elk, and other game. There were people everywhere. Surely this was the main camp. Just as speedily as they had left, the three scouts returned to the temporary camp upstream. They could see the hunters returning to camp as Pretty Eagle called to Top of the Mountain. "*Hummishi!*"

70

Without dismounting, Top of the Mountain let go the familiar coyote call of the returning scout! Again there was a flurry of activity as the camp prepared for the ceremonial "return of the scouts." This time there would be no pile of buffalo chips and no striking of the scouts. It was a glorious occasion, nonetheless, as singing was everywhere:

> The camp is in sight . . .
> the home camp *[chuuleekissuuk]*.

Red Bear's directions were clear and sharp as he did his own announcing: "We will move downstream close to the main camp. Gather meat on the way. When we arrive at the campsite, those of you who accomplished deeds against the enemy gather wood. We will have a good one tonight."

As night fell, an imposing pile of wood was quickly gathered, there being so many who had devastated the enemy. Soon there was spirited singing and dancing, which would last most of the night. The bonfire was huge and crackling. It was grand. Nothing was unpleasant everywhere you looked. Red Bear called to Top of the Mountain and Pretty Eagle, the two heroes.

"Your third member's foot is still badly swollen. You two go to the camp. Steal into camp *[ashduucheepdaala]*. Don't be found out. Learn all you can and return promptly and report." Top of the Mountain and Pretty Eagle were soon on their way. Preparations had not delayed these two experienced warriors of the war party trail. Soon they were stealing into their own camp. Each wore his blanket high as to quickly cover the lower part of the face if they encountered family or friends. Just as stealthily as if they were in an enemy camp, they hurriedly made their way toward a huge bonfire that lit up the sky. As they stood there contemplating their next move, they heard the singing.

> I have a man-friend,
> he is poor [has no honors].
> I want you for my husband, so it will be.

The song is one used in celebration of a victorious homecoming. Unmistakably, there was a full-fledged victory celebration right in the middle of camp! This was such a joyous and lively celebration, the two looked at each other in wonder. They had to find out, soon. Dawn would not be long and there was much to do before the Morning Star would be high in the sky.

Top of the Mountain led the way to his camp. His father's prized horse was picketed right in front of the lodge entrance. They could not do anything. Their entry into their own camp had to be kept a secret. It was Top of the Mountain who suggested the next move. "I have been seeing this woman for some time. She is almost as if she were my wife, too. Her husband is probably at the dance."

"Let's go," Pretty Eagle said.

Top of the Mountain stealthily peered into the woman's lodge through a lodge-pin opening. She was lying on a pillow at the edge of the fire, warming the bottoms of her feet, about to fall asleep. "She's in there. I will go off a ways and come back to let her know that I am here."

Pretty Eagle placed himself at the lodge-pin opening and kept his eye trained on the lodge's interior. Top of the Mountain approached and coughed audibly a few times before he tiptoed to Pretty Eagle's side.

"You rascal, she knows you are here." She raised up, stretched, and moved to the edge of the lodge's interior until her head rested against the skin lodge covering. She clasped her hands behind her head and leaned against the lodge covering. Top of the Mountain had broken off the long stem of a rye grass stalk. He probed the stem through a stitch hole of the lodge covering and nudged the back of her head. She closed the index and middle finger around the stem, out of sight of everyone in the lodge. As she clasped the stem, Top of the Mountain pulled on it repeatedly, beckoning her to come. She raised again and stretched.

"Grandmother, I should have gone outside a long time ago. Now I will go," she announced.

She came out quickly, and as she was getting accustomed to the dark, Top of the Mountain called to her from among some horses, which were standing a ways from the lodge. As they came together in an embrace, she stood on his feet. The ground was cold and her feet were bare. She threw both arms around his neck and pressed her body tightly to his and buried her face in his formidable chest. She hugged him tightly, even more than she had ever embraced her husband.

"You have returned. I will tell no one. What is it?"

"What's going on over there?" Top of the Mountain asked. "It is some sort of celebration about a victory or something? Your brother-in-law's name was mentioned in some of the praise songs, but I don't know what it's all about." She explained.

Top of the Mountain pressed his body to hers repeatedly, but they did not talk much. She knew nothing, this one, as if in a real daze. Further questioning did not reveal any more.

"We will come into camp tomorrow, you will see."

With that, the two stealthy heroes left her. Then, Pretty Eagle said, "I have a woman like that. Let's go find her."

They repeated the same process at her camp. Boy, did this one know things! She knew everything about everything. She was a veritable talking machine. What a woman, this one. Words poured out. She was talking to Pretty Eagle as she stood on his feet with her bare feet.

There was a wood-gathering party that stumbled onto a war party along the river. In the fight, the five men of the war party were wiped out, to one man in the wood-gathering party. The celebration was traditional to celebrate the victory. The heroes were being honored and it seemed that the entire camp was swept up in the glorious celebration. Her own husband was at the celebration. She asked Pretty Eagle, "Who is that with you over there?"

He replied, "That is Top of the Mountain."

She finally slowed down a little. "Oh, his brother-in-law struck coup as it had never been struck before. He was shot through the bicep but he is over there at the celebration. What are you two doing here? You were with the Red Bear war party against the Shoshones. Only heroes sneak back into their own camp on their return. What did you do?"

Pretty Eagle was brief as he told her, "Top of the Mountain over there struck coup. They designated the lodge farthest upstream as coup. I struck that. The last lodge downstream was also designated. Old Alligator struck that one. We wiped out and devastated their seventeen lodges. There are countless captives. We have their horses. We did not suffer any losses. Tomorrow you will see. You can go and tell them now."

"*Tell them?* What do you mean?" she asked in surprise. "If they are told, we will be found out! The nerve, tell them indeed! They beat us bad at the Red Lodge; it's good that you humiliated them," she added. They stole out of camp as suddenly as they had come and soon arrived at the war-party camp.

Top of the Mountain would laughingly later recall the night to young men of the tribe. He admonished them, "These seemingly know-nothing women are the cleverest of beings, clever beyond the capacity of any man. Don't ever be a jealous husband."

The grand homecoming of Red Bear's war party was now in full and glorious swing! The Morning Star was high. Dawn was very close. With deliberate haste, they departed for the main camp.

> When I go searching,
> I will go right in front,
> Nothing will ever,
> can ever . . .

Spotted Horse trailed off with loud and happy whoops that echoed through the woods and along the river. He was magnificent in full regalia as he lifted his rich voice in glorious song! The weasel tails and hair locks of his war [chief] shirt seemed to cover every bit of his formidable and awesome body. [Weasel tails and hair locks on war shirts denote the deeds of the wearer. They are worn as proud badges of war deeds. A profusion of weasel tails and hair locks was prominent as Spotted Horse came forth in all his greatness.]

Up until now, Spotted Horse had been uncharacteristically quiet and inhibited. He did this deliberately, lest he be compared with Red Bear and thereby diminish the leadership of the Great One. The two were equally renowned as champions of the tribe. The inclination to compare them was always there. He had been careful not to detract attention from Red Bear. Now as his song echoed through the woods this early dawn, Spotted Horse did not contain himself any longer. All eyes were on this proud and imposing figure, as Red Bear suppressed a smile with an understanding that could be shared only by these two Great Ones.

Only a few women here and there had arisen in the main camp. Some were just lighting fires to start the day. Otherwise, the camp was quiet in restful sleep following the celebrating of the night before.

Loud and sharp volleys of gunfire broke the still of the early morning as weapons were fired in the air! There was a profusion of voices raised as high and as loud as had ever been heard. The horse herd was driven into the middle of camp. Captives were everywhere and from a corner of the camp, the victorious war party burst into the circle of white lodges. There was no doubt. Victory and revenge was ours! Red Bear had returned!

Everywhere there was confused excitement. Women not yet fully dressed came running as they groped for legging ties [garters]. Some were running with their leg coverings [stockings] around the ankles, grappling with half-donned apparel as they came running out to witness the event that had been on the minds of so many for so long! There in the lead, far ahead of everyone, was Top of the Mountain.

His woman was slightly in front of him, where he had placed her. She wore a reddish dress with the top part around the shoulder darkened till it was a dark, deep blue. With her dark hair and stocky build, many in the Crow camp thought her to be a Shoshone woman. He was the unmistakable hero. He brandished a shiny rifle as he led the procession at a brisk gallop!

At a modest distance behind him rode Pretty Eagle, striker of the second coup. Still behind Pretty Eagle rode Old Alligator, all by himself and looking every bit the great hero that he was! The rest followed with Shoshone captives liberally mixed in with the charging and victorious procession. As people wordlessly searched for them, Red Bear and Spotted Horse entered the circle from another quarter, riding abreast with Woman on Earth on the sorrel paint slightly to the left and ahead of Red Bear. The two veteran warriors were magnificent in full regalia! As they galloped, their weasel tails and deed markers seemed to bounce in unison. Who would dare to venture in front of these two? It was a magnificent sight. Top of the Mountain had never before known the exultation he now felt. As he looked about, everything he saw was pleasing. If there was anything unpleasant this day, Top of the Mountain was not aware of it as he savored this glorious entry into the legends and stories of the Crows.

Just as suddenly as it had entered the circle of camp, the war party ended the dancing and singing to disappear into the milling and happy crowd. It could have gone on all day. As Top of the Mountain made his way to his father's lodge with his bride, he did not know that for generations his name would grace the lips of the Crows, time and time again, along with the name of Red Bear. He did not know that his story of this day would be retold with Red Bear's revenge!

Elusive Fame and Glory

The Story of Spotted Horse *[Iichiilixaxxish]*

Fame, glory, and respect are elusive and fleeting in the Crow way of life. The system can be very liberal as it places elements of respect and honor upon tribal members, but it can also be extremely demanding and unforgiving. The tribal ethic is precise to the extreme, although there is a variety of ways through which fame, glory, and respect can be earned and appropriately articulated in tribal terms. The ethic can almost appear fickle as respect is first bestowed, then withdrawn. Ethics of the Crow system are unique, quite unlike anything anywhere else. They are different because they are uniquely Crow.

HIS YOUTH—GAINING A NAME FOR HIMSELF

The story of Spotted Horse is told in several versions, ranging from proud accounts of his many accomplishments to those accounts that are told in reserved and hushed tones. In any case, his story is one that will survive the years and ages of the Crows.

Spotted Horse was not a childhood name. It was not a name given him through the tribe, although he was born to a woman of the River Crows band. The River Crows frequented the Yellowstone and Musselshell areas of present-day Montana and from there often visited the parent tribe of the Crows, the North Dakota Gros Ventre or Hidatsa. Of the bands of the Crows, the River Crows were the ones who exchanged most visits with the Hidatsa. These exchanges were by individuals and groups and sometimes extended into long periods of visitation, termed going to "live with them." It was during one of these visits that a fine boy was born to one of the River Crow women. He was "white," having light eyes and an extremely fair complexion with light-colored hair. He was different from other Crow children.

Children, often being cruel and quick to note differences between themselves and others, dubbed him with names like "That One Who Is Different," "That One Who Is Hidatsa," "That One Who Is Not a Crow," "That One Who Is Not One of Us," and other unkind names that reflected his fairness of complexion and his not being born among the Crows. Even as he was growing up, the angular and powerful physique, which would set him apart from other men later on, was already apparent. He quickly excelled at things that boys of his age did and proved to be strong and a fast runner. His strength and quickness developed quickly and improved as he grew older until he was a young man even before his time. Still, the unkind names persisted until his grandfather became concerned. Badger with a Hump on the Neck *[Awachii Appuush Xishish]* was his grandfather, and he had powerful medicine [powers]. This grandfather had fasted on the Castle Rocks of the Pryor Mountains and had been blessed with a visitation by the Outcasts.[1] The Outcasts had bestowed powerful and unique powers to Badger with a Hump on the Neck. He now called the grandson to his side.

"You are now a young man. You should be enjoying respect from your peers and your tribe, but that has not been. You do not even have a respected name. It is time that you enjoy good things. I am going to make a man out of you, a real man, one that people will be proud to know."

With his own unique ritual and ceremony, Badger with a Hump on the Neck bestowed some of his supernatural powers on the young grandson with appropriate bundle and ritual. Even though he was only an early teenager, the young man joined a war party that was going into the Big Horn Basin country, a land frequently challenged by the enemies of the Crows to the south, the Shoshones and Arapahos. As the Crow war party was making its way, it was suddenly attacked by a large force of Arapahos. There was soon a running battle, with the Arapahos in hot pursuit. There was still no pitched battle, and the Crows had not organized any form of resistance when the young man reined in his horse and dismounted. He got down right in the path of the attacking Arapahos!

This totally surprised his Crow companions, but the attacking Arapahos were incredulous at the sight of this Crow who dared to take frontal ground in the very path of their attack! The race for honors, to be first to strike him, was furious. It seemed to him that there were so many horsemen bearing down on him that there was no target. He took a few steps back and took aim with his rifle on the leading horseman, who leaned off to his left. This agile man on a shiny black horse then cut in front of the others and struck him with a resounding "Haa-heh!" Just then he fired the double-shot load harmlessly and aimlessly into the horde. The smoke from the gun enveloped both rider and the boy. He did not panic. He immediately reversed the rifle and used it as a club and struck one of the riders, nearly unseating him from his horse. The two struggled briefly for the reins of the Arapaho's horse until repeated blows rained on the boy from the right, the left, and from behind him. He was surrounded!

Now the Crows could see that he was trapped. He swung whatever he could lay his hands on, the gun having been wrested from his grasp. He wrenched a loaded rifle from an attacker and as he pointed it first this way, then turning and pointing it the other way, he cleared a sizable patch of ground for himself. Now he could maneuver, but gun smoke and the swirling dust obscured the vision of the Crows who were regrouping and reorganizing for a counterattack as they turned and looked for him.

"I can't see him anymore! They got him! No! There he is—hanging on to the tail of the white horse and fighting with the rider!"

These and other shouts and war whoops filled the air as the Crows mounted their warhorses. They readied their weapons as they whipped their horses to the attack. As the Crows approached the swirling mass of horses, dust, and men, the young man strode manfully out of the din and melee! He was safe. Beaten badly, with an indescribable collection of cuts and bruises, still the boy was safe! No bullets had penetrated his body and he was on his own two feet! What a man! What an exhibition of valor and bravery!

Even as the pitched battle between the Arapahos and Crows continued, Crow after Crow came to admire him and to heap praise and comforting words upon the badly battered but happy young man, happy that he was alive and back with his people. He had had a good horse and good weapons when the attack was unleashed by the Arapahos, but now as the battle ended in a standoff, he did not have a thing with him. The Arapahos had taken everything he had, everything except what could not be physically taken away by anyone.

He had struck first coup! He was the hero! He had been subjected to what is called *ditch ooliok!* He was struck at least four times. They took turns to strike him. He was struck simultaneously and at least four times. He escaped certain death!

The boy was afforded appropriate honors when the war party returned to the Crow camp on the Yellowstone as word raced from one end of the camp to the other about his stand, his being struck over and over again and being first to strike the Arapahos. His grandfather was proudly satisfied, but he knew that it was not done.

It was not long thereafter that the Crows were camped near what is the confluence of the Ashkish shipuo[2] [what is now the Clark's Fork River] and the Elk River [Yellowstone River]. From the outer sentries, to the horse herders, and into the main camp, the word was flashed, "Some people are approaching; they come in peace!" Leaders from the camp, warriors, and camp police hurried out to meet the group some distance from the fringes of the camp, but still in full sight of the curious, who even walked from the camp circle to gaze at the two groups coming together. The leader of the group was a tall, handsome Arapaho, mounted on a shiny black beauty of a gelding. It was he who did most of the talking through sign and interpreters.

"We come in peace. We do not wish to do battle. We will not bother your camp, your horses, nor do we desire your possessions. There was a recent Crow war party that we attacked. Even before the battle was joined and while we were still in pursuit, a young man dismounted. He dismounted although his horse was still fresh. We could not kill him, we could not bring him down, and he withstood all of our attacks. My name is Spotted Horse. I gained honors by striking him first. It is that young man whom we wish to see. We are curious as to what sort of a person he is. It is he that we wish to see."

The group was brought into the circle of the camp, where much food was served in a feast and the young man brought forth to face his attackers, this time in the safety and tranquility of a camp at peace for now. Again, it was the leader who spoke.

"My name is Spotted Horse. This black is my horse. Both my horse and I are well known among the tribes to the south of you. Listen, you Crows, and hear me well. From this day forward, call this boy Spotted Horse. I give him my name. I give him my horse also. So be it."

Praise songs echoed throughout the camp. The name Spotted Horse was repeated in praise over and over again. It was now a Crow name. The grandfather was happy and satisfied. With his new name and his newfound respect and adulation within the tribe, it would be related later that for all the young men in the tribe, there was no equal of Spotted Horse.

As he embarked on vision quests, making living flesh and other offerings, he gained more and more favor with patron spirits. He did sundances and all things that young men do to gain power and blessing. [Such rituals were undeniable keys to prominence and prestige in the tribe.] It is said that Spotted Horse's chest, shoulders, and back were covered with scars from self-inflicted cuts and gouges [offerings] and sundance pierce wounds. He acquired more power, demonstrating it again and again until he was recognized as truly one of the Great Ones. Spotted Horse's greatness began with his encounter with his "Arapaho friends," but it was in an encounter with the Sioux while he was with the Kicked in the Bellies (a clan within the Crows) that his invulnerability to enemy weapons was firmly established.

A sizable Sioux war party had been chased into some outcropping rocks by warriors from the Kicked in the Belly clan. The Sioux fashioned a fortification from which they had a commanding sweep with gunfire around the periphery. From the fortification, the Sioux held out for four days and four nights, yet they could not escape and the Crows could not breach the fence or rout them from its protection. Crow after Crow made "bravery runs" toward the fence, only to be driven off by the withering fire of the besieged warriors. Fires would be started to rout them, only to be doused by sudden and heavy rain.

Among the Crows word was out, "Don't take unnecessary chances. Don't be foolish. They may hurt some of you, even by accident. They are no ordinary foe. Give them a wide berth."

It was on the fourth day that some River Crows arrived on the scene, Spotted Horse and his grandfather among them. Badger with a Hump on the Neck told his grandson, "This is what I prepared you for. Go and do it." Spotted Horse did not hesitate. He quickly donned the unclean-looking fringed shirt commonly associated with the Outcasts, took his weapon, and was ready. He sang his medicine song. It was short, having only three parts. His grandfather told the Kicked in the Bellies, "He is going in. He will rout them. Follow at your will and at your risk, but follow him." Spotted Horse did not rein to the right or to the left. He gave the black his head as man and horse plunged straight ahead.

The Sioux had been sleepless for four nights but secure in their cover. They were sleepy and had now become slightly complacent. Spotted Horse crashed through the fence and right into the midst of the embattled Sioux. There was complete bedlam and chaos as the fence became alive with gun smoke and flying shot wads. As he half-fell, half-jumped off his horse, Spotted Horse impaled a tall Sioux to the ground with his lance, which was fashioned from elk antlers. The rout was in full and frightful progression up and down the barricade as Crows and Sioux met in hand-to-hand combat in the midst of frantic gunfire, shouting, screaming, and yelling. In a messy, muddy few moments it was over. The Sioux were routed and wiped out. Spotted Horse had taken numerous guns; he had crashed through the fence and had struck first coup! The Kicked in the Belly camp buzzed with accounts of the victory. Spotted Horse was untouched by the enemy's bullets and weapons. He was unscathed!

Still he gained more and more mystical and supernatural powers to add to those already bestowed upon him by his grandfather. This continued until he became a man to be feared and a good man to have on your side. Crows seemed to heed and abide by his every wish and even his every word.

It was against the Sioux that Spotted Horse led a war party. His instructions were short and to the point. He said, "On this journey, be kind to creatures of the bird world. Even if it is a tiny bird, be kind to it. Do not harm or frighten even one of them." It happened without any warning and there was no time to think about it. A small bird, with its wings fluttering wildly and rapidly, came straight toward a young man's face. He saw the bird from a corner of his eye. Instinctively, he lashed out with his quirt, knocking the tiny bird to the ground. He jumped off his horse, picked up the small feathered form, and blew repeatedly on its abdomen to revive it. It was too late; the tiny bird was dead. The young man was still holding the lifeless form in the palm of his hand when Spotted Horse approached. He already knew what had happened. He did not raise his voice and he showed neither anger nor disappointment, although it was difficult for him. He said, "You would do well to turn around right here now and go home. You will be killed."

With obvious disappointment and trying to cover his shame, the young man replied, "I will come anyway, but I will not go near the action. I will watch from a distance and not take part. I will not go home from here." Spotted Horse reined his horse around to return to the head of the procession as he said, "All right, you come, but you will be killed."

When the Sioux were engaged, everything went well for the war party. Spotted Horse completed another of the required deeds. He led a successful war party. There was only one blemish: the young man who had killed the bird was unexplainably killed by the Sioux, even though he had watched from a distance in the pitched battle following the taking of horses by the Crows.

Crows pause and review many things from time to time. Sometimes they ask: "Who are the greatest? Let us name four of the greatest—only the greatest and only four!" When it comes to miraculous things that Crows did, invariably Spotted Horse and his scaling of the tower of buffalo chips [in "The Saga of Red Bear"] is named. His power and greatness were awesome, but still comparisons were made. They would say, "Sure, Spotted Horse is truly great, but what about the others? What about Red Bear?"

RED BEAR AND SPOTTED HORSE

Whenever the Great Ones of the tribe are discussed and compared, two names invariably come up without fail, Red Bear and Spotted Horse. These two outstanding ones are so similar in many respects, yet so different in their own way that it was always difficult to single out which was truly the greatest. It was so difficult to define that there was no consensus, yet still the comparisons of the two were constantly on the mind of the Crows who witnessed their grandeur.

In the meantime, as befitted Great Ones who were disdainful of petty things and issues, Spotted Horse and Red Bear did not lend dignity to the comparing process. They just would not become involved and went about their own ways. They had been together when Red Bear led the war party to avenge the loss of the Red Lodge party. On that occasion, there was considerable desire to compare the two Great Ones, but they managed to avoid any sort of open rivalry. In fact, Spotted Horse went to great lengths to avoid the limelight while Red Bear successfully ravaged the Shoshone camp, "wiping out the seventeen lodges." There was considerable desire and effort to compare them, but Spotted Horse just would not do anything that would detract from Red Bear's leadership. Even when the war party returned to camp, the two Great Ones put on a glorious exhibition of togetherness and loyalty, displaying no rivalry whatever.

Without openly stating the issue, people were given to wondering which of the two giants possessed the greater power, known and unknown. The question persisted, but it would be submerged by principles of the tribe, which included the premise that if one had great supernatural powers, it was necessary to use care when employing those powers:

> Do not use that power against your own. To do so might result in bad and even terrible things to come to you and your loved ones.

Still, efforts to compare Red Bear and Spotted Horse persisted. The Crows did not rest; they just had to know which was the greater.

Hand-game is an age-old game that is still played by the Crows today. It is a game in which there is heavy betting as one team is pitted against another. It is at once a game of skill, cunning, and no small amount of "medicine." The most skilled players will not go into a game without considerable backup with medicine, starting with the medicine man and extending even to lesser team members to support their endeavors and skill. Teams will even go outside of their ranks to invoke power and blessing through people with medicine.

The Greasy Mouth and Whistle Water clans were engaged in a challenge game this day. The best players from both clans were pitted against each other in a one-decision-winner-take-all game that captured the attention of the entire camp. Even the singers and supporting players were the best that could be mustered for this all-important challenge game to see which was the better, the Greasy Mouths or the Whistle Water. The betting exceeded anything that had been seen until then. Both sides brought horses, blankets, weapons, and all things of value to bet. These would be matched item for item with bets from the other side. As an added precaution and to ensure that they would win, the Whistle Waters seated Red Bear to watch over and be guardian of the clan's bets. The Greasy Mouths, not to be outdone, seated Spotted Horse to guard their bets. Each side now had a Great One to guard its bets. Who would even try to take anything away from Red Bear or Spotted Horse?

After the ceremonial test to see who would score first, the game began with an audience bigger than any audience to observe a single hand-game in the memory of those who were there. Spotted Horse looked across at his fellow Great One, who was now unmistakably in an adversary position. Red Bear made no pretense about the gravity and importance of the occasion. He had brought his pipe, and this he lit up and blew smoke in the direction of the Greasy Mouths, their bets, and Spotted Horse. This was serious!

It was no longer a game of fun, and the entire camp watched to see which clan would win. Spotted Horse had brought his pipe, too, and he lit it. He exchanged puff for puff with Red Bear as the two powerful ones unabashedly and without any reservation invoked powers to turn the game in their own favor. The singing and cheering was deafening as the two teams seesawed in advantage. Still the two Great Ones smoked and smoked, blowing smoke across the heavy air that now hung over this all-important game. It would seem that one team had the advantage and would win, only to see the other side rise and turn the tide. This went on and the tide turned again and again. When it appeared that the game would go on forever, the Greasy Mouths hit a streak and won. The Whistle Waters were beaten!

The Greasy Mouths could not contain their elation, pride, and joy. The vanquished Whistle Waters sat in their places, with heads down, waiting for the victors to complete their celebrating so that all could feast. The Greasy Mouths had beaten the very best that the Whistle Waters had put together. Pride, cheering, and jeering welled over! Humiliation of the Whistle Waters led to arrogance!

"Have Water Edge tell of his deeds for us. He is a Greasy Mouth. Flaunt the Whistle Waters with tales they could never match! Let them listen to Greasy Mouth greatness in humbleness. Come, Water Edge, tell of your deeds for us, the victorious Greasy Mouths!" Water Edge came forward and picked up a burning firebrand from the cooking fire. As he brandished it for all to see, he began:

"*Huuk a he!* I was in deep sleep and relishing restful and deep sleep one night when the enemy 'shot down on me.' I jumped up and it was this firebrand that I picked up. Sparks flew in every direction as I unmistakably struck first coup. It was with this that I struck real and undisputed first coup!" He put the firebrand down and picked up another.

"*Huuk a he!* I was sleeping peacefully and in deep rest another night when the enemy 'shot down on me.' I got up and picked up this firebrand. With the still-flaming embers, I struck undeniable first coup with it. It was with this!" He put that firebrand down and picked up still another.

"H*uuk a he!* Still another night, I was deep in peaceful and restful sleep when the enemy 'shot down on me.' Unabashed, I jumped up, picked this up and struck sure first coup with it!" Again, he returned the firebrand to the fire and picked up still another.

"*Huuk a he!* Still another night, I was sleeping peacefully, when again the enemy dared to charge in on me and 'shoot down on me.' I arose just as I was, picked this up, and struck first coup with it like it had never been struck before. It was with this." For the fourth time, he returned a firebrand to the cooking fire. He unsheathed his large-bladed knife, which glistened in the bright sunshine. As he brandished the bright, shiny, and ever sharp blade, he was at full voice.

"*Huuk a he!* On yet another night, I was sleeping peacefully when the enemy 'shot down on me.' I got up and struck first coup with this." He waved the blade for all to see.

As the Greasy Mouths extended their celebration into a near frenzy, the humiliated Whistle Waters could only force crooked grins and attempt small talk among themselves. It was inevitable and now it had happened. Red Bear and Spotted Horse had been pitted against each other. Spotted Horse had emerged the victor, even overshadowing the players on both sides who were directly involved in the challenge hand-game [names of the hand-game players and their roles are not remembered]. Word of the hand-game and how Spotted Horse had emerged victorious raced through the camp and from band to band of the Crows. Soon all the Crows knew. No amount of denial would ever submerge the rivalry between these two Great Ones. Not now. Not ever. Would Red Bear get even? Would he try? What if he did? What would Spotted Horse do?

It was springtime and the runoff was almost complete. The camp was at its biggest before war parties and hunting parties would diminish and reduce the numbers of people in the Crow camp. It was a time when clubs, societies, and clans enjoyed full membership, and spirits were high. It was wife-taking time! Rival clubs, like the Foxes and Lumpwoods, tried to outdo each other and humiliate one another by taking wives from the rival group. Even clans heightened their sometimes not-so-friendly rivalries. Wife taking was occurring even among the clans. In hushed tones, the word was all over the camp. Red Bear had taken the wife of a Greasy Mouth! In the Greasy Mouth camps, there was quiet indignation and confused muttering. They would ask, "What can we do? What measure of retribution can we exact on him?" The aggrieved husband was asked, "Are you angry? Do you want revenge?" He replied, "Of course I am angry and hurt. I wish deep revenge, but what can I do against Red Bear? He is all powerful and has strong medicine. What sort of revenge am I capable of bringing on him?"

High Swan was a young Greasy Mouth. He was handsome and was known to have a way with women, always in demand at socials and dances. He was truly a future prominent member of the tribe. It was High Swan who came to the aggrieved husband. "Are you truly angry? Do you really want revenge?" he asked. The husband answered, "Look, she was my wife. I loved and cherished her. Of course I am angry. Of course I want revenge." High Swan boldly pronounced the feeling of the Greasy Mouths: "Red Bear is not the only one who is a man. Just because of his great power, he thinks that he can continue to do anything he wants with immunity. That cannot be so. We shall see. He is not one without nights. He has to go into the dark of night and drop his defenses, too. Just like anybody else. It will be so."

The next morning, Red Bear's Number One Wife was gone from his lodge and camp! High Swan had taken her in the same manner as a mongrel dog sneaks into camp and snatches a choice morsel in the quiet of the night.

It was not long thereafter in the springtime that Red Bear victoriously and gloriously returned from a war party against the Sioux. He brought back countless horses. There was a Sioux horse renowned among the tribes. It was a horse frequently in the center of discussion and fantasy among the Crows. The horse was called a "pinto-neck," and he could not have been a better-constructed horse had he been sculpted. He was a beautiful horse, prized by all who saw or knew him. Now as Red Bear paraded around the camp circle singing victory songs *[chuut daak]*, he rode the pinto-neck. What a sight to behold! The pinto-neck would prance, jump in place a few times, and then go forward in a series of short side jumps. What a sight! One wondered which was more impressive, the man or the horse, but surely the two together.

The Greasy Mouths camped in a group toward the rear center of the camp circle. Spotted Horse's camp was situated in the midst of the Greasy Mouth encampment. As Red Bear made his glorious round to where he was, even with the Greasy Mouths and Spotted Horse, he suddenly turned sullen and disdainful.

"Oh, there are some poor, pitiful, and little people here [having no honors]. I didn't even see them. I could have stepped on them, they are so low!" Red Bear said.

Spotted Horse did not miss a word of the cutting remarks. He uncovered his pipe, took the pipe stem, and scored it with his ever sharp knife. Spotted Horse then took the pipe stem and broke it so that it had a sharp-splintered end. This he stuck in the ground with a brief ritual and said, "If he gets as far as the opening of the camp to the east without mishap and without embarrassment, then what I do with my medicine is not true." The Greasy Mouths who were witnesses to the events of the moment watched anxiously as Red Bear resumed his victorious and glorious circling of the camp, singing all the way. He was almost out of the circle of the camp and was approaching the opening of the camp on the east side. From an unseen place from the rear of a row of lodges, a dog sprang from where it was lying and appeared to be jumping into the air to become airborne as he barklessly charged Red Bear and the pinto-neck.

The dog's ears were laid back as it raced with bared teeth at the regal man and horse, not yet making a sound. Just as the horse saw the dog, the dog lunged for his snout with a loud, guttural growl that came from the depths of the chest. The magnificent horse planted its hind feet and pushed off with its front feet as it twisted and reared to escape the sudden and growling menace. Red Bear did not lose his seat, but in a fraction of a moment he was standing on the ground astride the now helpless pinto-neck. It had broken its back right at the hipbone. As Red Bear stood there with a bewildered look on his face, his prize of a horse that, but a moment ago, was prancing proudly through the camp was destroyed on the spot. No one cheered.

Red Bear and Spotted Horse had at last pitted their tremendous powers against each other to the astonishment of all who witnessed this expected—but surprising—turn of events. The two giants had openly targeted the other with their supernatural powers and Spotted Horse had won. Or had he?

That question occupied the minds of those who knew the two Great Ones and their emerging rivalry. Would Red Bear let the issue rest here? Would there be another occasion on which one or the other would be subject to the fearful wrath of these two adversaries from the same tribe? What would be the consequences?

WHERE SPOTTED HORSE FOUGHT—A
MONUMENT (*IICHIILI XAXXISH ANMAAWULUA*)

Horseracing is another age-old and popular pastime of the Crows. Owning, training, and racing good horses is a lifelong ambition of any Crow worthy of the name. Crow men would go to great lengths and perform extraordinary measures to acquire and to own good horses. They would even defy death to acquire horses, it being a measure leading to chieftainship. So it was that horseracing remained a high and rewarding endeavor, and does so even to this day.

Before racetracks, horseracing among the Crows was on the straightaway and match races were the mode. There would be two or more sides, each group supporting a particular horse or any number of horses. Horses were matched in a variety of contests, from short sprints to distance endurance events. The finish line was always "where the crowd was."

In endurance races, markers would be placed some distance from where the crowd was. The racers would begin the race at the finish line, race to the marker, turn around it, and race back to where the crowd was. A popular practice in distance races was to station "whippers-from-the-rear" [helpers] along the racecourse. As the racehorse began to tire or falter, the whippers would come up and help urge the horse along by whipping it from behind.

Where the crowd was was always the center of activity. It was here that matches were made and bets placed. Bettors, spectators, jockeys, horse owners, and others were found here, milling around during and between races. It was a grand event. Chiefs, Great Ones, and everyone of note was here to lend dignity and meaning to the event. It was an occasion that Crows did not want to miss. They had to be here. It was a good time to see which horses were the best in a given race. The best horses of the tribe would be here. People wore their best clothes, rode their best horses, and led other prized horses. These would be bet on the races. They also carried good weapons, blankets, and other possessions of value. These would be bet, as there was no money as we know it today.

Spotted Horse had a younger brother. His name was *"Kaaxu Cheete"* [Goes Into a Frenzy Often, Goes Into Delirium Often, or Frequently Loses Sobriety. For purposes of this story, he will be called "Frenzies Often" or just "Frenzies"]. Frenzies was a poor man [having no honors]. He belonged in the lower elements of the Crow system. Although he was comfortable with a good home and good family, he knew his place. He was pitiable and poor in the eyes of his people. He harbored no ill will to anyone and was a threat to no one in any endeavor. He was justly proud of his big brother, Spotted Horse, whom he idolized.

It was midsummer and the Crows were camped along *Bilap chaashe*[3] [what is now the Powder River]. Horses had good grass and now were showing good flesh and good condition. Shiny, muscular horses were everywhere, evidencing the keen and meticulous training that was a part of every Crow man's labors. It was horseracing time, and the camp was alive with horsemen leading prized horses, horses they would race or bet; sometimes with their favorite jockeys riding double with them, aspiring horsemen worked diligently as they readied their mounts for the races, each wishing that his horse would be featured. This was a good day to gain new and lasting prestige. Still others, like Frenzies, went about menial and lower-level tasks, making sure that the regal ones, the Great Ones, were given a wide berth and enjoyed good vantage points as benefited their stature and position.

The chiefs, Great Ones, and other renowned men took their customary places of honor. Their exalted positions and role as prominent men dictated that they not lower themselves to mix too freely with other elements, although they would tactfully go about the area of "where the crowd was," casually place bets, and return almost to a disdainful distance from others not of their cut. It was fashion to return from these occasions and relate that "I saw [so and so], one of the Great Ones. He was every inch a chief. He was so much a chief that he would hardly open his eyes, as if oblivious to all that was going on around him." The role of the chief was not like that of a king or hierarchical position that immediately comes to mind. Rather, the Great Ones were considered to be above the happenings and concerns of everyday life because they occupied such an important role in the tribal lifestyle. Their leadership was not one determined by lineage or even selection of peers, but by proving that they were fearless and willing to sacrifice for the tribe. Such bravery and duty was essential to the tribal way of life. But this distinction did not put them in a position in which it was acceptable to belittle the members of the tribe without honors or prestige; it would be an abuse of power and without honor to do so, as those were the people to whom the Great Ones were expected to be most compassionate.

"They had class," onlookers might say. Spotted Horse was unmistakably of this caliber. He took his place with the Great Ones and chiefs. From there he would occasionally venture to where the bets were being taken and leave after his wager had been placed. The horses were good and the races were spirited and exciting. It came to the point where one race seemed to be more outstanding in spirit and feeling than the one before. As it happened, two great horses were matched and betting began and continued at a brisk pace. All things of value were being placed on one side as with the other. Later, these would be matched item for item by the sponsors, if not by the bettors themselves. Spotted Horse took his prized horse and bet it without matching it with a corresponding horse from the other side. He returned to his usual place to watch the race. It was an exciting race.

The horse that Spotted Horse had bet on put up a good race, but the horse from the other side put up a better run at the finish and won. There was cheering on one side and disappointment on the other. Spotted Horse was particularly disappointed over the loss. His gaze wandered somewhat and then came to where his prized horse had been tethered. It had been matched with another horse from the other side with the halter ropes tied together so that the winner could take both horses. As he looked at the two horses tied together, Frenzies came to claim them. It was he who had bet the other horse, and the two bet horses were now tied together. Spotted Horse kicked his black into a brisk trot and as he approached, Frenzies was already picking up the halter ropes to take his winnings. Frenzies was grinning as the Great One said, "Frenzies, that is my horse."

"I know," Frenzies said. "He was yours." He began to lead him away. Spotted Horse persisted and became so insistent that Frenzies not take his winnings that they began to attract a growing audience, which now hung on every word between the Great One and his brother. It got increasingly heated and Spotted Horse began to shout and uncharacteristically assume a most menacing demeanor. This was unheard of! The Great One was "casting sour grapes" all around and threatening his little brother. No one could have ever imagined what happened next, not even in the wildest of situations! Frenzies was beginning to lead the horses away, having been equally insistent that they were now his, when Spotted Horse slid off his horse and through clenched teeth, muttered: *"You keep doing what you should not be doing! You have to be taught a lesson! A lesson you will never forget! now see what i will do to you!"*

Spotted Horse had looped his quirt around his wrist as he slid off his horse, and now this fearsome giant of a man made the air whistle as he brought the quirt painfully down on the cowering Frenzies. Spotted Horse lost all control as he whipped and lashed his smaller brother. There were loud pops as the heavy quirt broke clothing and skin, until Frenzies lay in a helpless and battered heap, feeling pain no more.

The crowd seemed afraid to move. They could not believe what they had just seen. The Great One, the one feared by friend and foe alike, feared even by the enemy from the tribes around the Crows, feared even by those who had not even seen this giant of a man who was a terror on the attack, had just beaten a "poor" man into a helpless heap! Worse than that, it was his own little brother! The little brother who idolized him and was quick to name him as his protector now lay bloodied and beaten at the hands of the great Spotted Horse! The Crows would pile a monument—rocks to mark the spot Where Spotted Horse Fought! It would be a perpetual reminder of the fleeting glory of a Great One.

The camp had moved again and Frenzies had already erected his camp and a good meal was ready. His wife came in and said, "Do you know who is out there, looking for a place to pitch his camp? It is Spotted Horse." Frenzies painfully walked outside, as his bruises and wounds were just now beginning to be painfully swollen and festering in the summer heat.

"Spotted Horse," he called. Spotted Horse looked over but did not speak. He repeated the call and bade him to come over and eat, then put up his camp afterward. Still, the giant just stood there, pondering this turn of events. In a louder voice, Frenzies called again, "Spotted Horse. Come and eat. It is your favorite food. You can set up camp afterward." Others could now hear and Spotted Horse dropped the pole ties he was carrying. He and his family went into Frenzies's lodge.

Even young boys already knew of the events that were on the lips of everyone. They would pretend to be playing and sneak up to Frenzies's lodge. They would then fall to the ground, lift up the bottom of the lodge, and peer in to see what was going on inside. There was the giant Spotted Horse relishing broiled steak and bone marrow that was served in the lodge of his brother who he had just beaten mercilessly. A loving, loyal brother who idolized him had forgiven Spotted Horse. The tribe did not.

Following the events of Where Spotted Horse Fought, it seemed that time and circumstances were returned to the time before the first encounter with the Arapahos. Spotted Horse still had his name, but no longer did it evoke awe, respect, and honor. It is told that old friends avoided him. Hardly anyone came to visit anymore. His advice and words, which were so eagerly sought before, no longer were heeded or wanted. People no longer came to him for aid, comfort, or protection. He no longer quickened the pulse when he appeared on the scene.

Even though an unforgiving system and ethic had all but reduced Spotted Horse to a nonentity, he did not quit. He did not stop trying. He could not stop. The strong heart, the iron will, and the furious intensity that motivated this giant of a man would not let him quit. He continued on the warpath over and over again, although no longer a leader or a respected champion. His reckless and fearsome ferocity remained unabated. He would not hesitate to attack whenever there was an opportunity, but praises were now subdued, spoken in a hushed tone.

It was about the same time of the seasons as in "The Saga of Red Bear." Snow banks and river ice were rapidly disappearing. Rivers, creeks, and even gullies were swollen with swirling, muddy, and ice-cold waters. Muddy and slushy patches were everywhere on the plains surrounding the Powder River as it wound its way into the chalky mud banks of the lower river.

It was early spring; the thaw and runoff were here. A sizable Crow war party was returning from a raid on the Sioux, with the enemy in hot and spirited pursuit. It seemed that the pursuing Sioux numbers were increasing every time the Crows crossed swollen waterways with the large herd of captured horses they were driving. As they crossed swollen waters, the Sioux would catch up rapidly. Groups of Crows repeatedly turned back and engaged the pursuing Sioux in pitched battles, giving the war party and the horse herd more time to negotiate swirling waters. When the horse herd was distant from the Sioux, the groups of Crows broke off the engagement to catch up with the war party. It seemed like every time this occurred, Spotted Horse was in the thickest of the melee and was almost always the last one to break off and return. Many times, Crows would look back and see the distinctive, laterally decorated leggings that Spotted Horse wore in battle. [Crow leggings are traditionally decorated longitudinally along the edge of the leggings, leaving the front part plain and undecorated. Spotted Horse wore Arapaho leggings that were laterally striped, which stood out among men with leggings.] As the numbers of

Sioux pursuers seemed ever larger, word was passed up and down the Crow ranks.

"We will go back and hold them a longer time. Cross as many coulees as you can. Cross two or maybe three channels. Then, we will catch up with you. Hurry!" Spotted Horse probably muttered to himself, "I will make sure of that."

The Crow horse herders now summoned additional help, driving the horse herd ever harder. There were loud and muddy splashes everywhere as horses were driven recklessly into rushing waters, with loud whoops and cracking whips filling the spring air above the noise of the angry streams. On a sloping plain between two coulees, the Crows met their pursuers head-on. The fury of their charge literally drove the Sioux back into the swollen gully they were still crossing. The Sioux were still mostly in the treacherous swift current and the battle was intense. Crows were riding hard back and forth along the swollen waters and from that advantage drove Sioux after Sioux downstream or back into the waters they were crossing. A major factor in the Crows holding the Sioux from the chase was the ever present figure of Spotted Horse. He seemed to be everywhere. His recklessness and furious abandon were inspiring to behold. He had not lost any of his battle skills nor any of his iron will.

The main body of Crows had crossed two streams and was readying to drive the horse herd across a third stream. As the Crows looked back at the sloping and muddy plain, the battle had been broken off. The rear guard was busy leaving the first stream and heading for the second one. The Sioux had abandoned the battleground and were about finished crossing the stream on their return to Sioux country. Only a few straggling Sioux were just barely still in the water or leaving it. The chase was over and so was the battle.

On the muddy plain lay the lifeless form of a giant of a man. One knee was propped up, with the striped Arapaho leggings standing out in plain sight even from that distance. Spotted Horse was dead. A legend had died at the hands of the Sioux through whom he had gained many honors. Even they did not linger to bother with his lifeless form.

The passing of Spotted Horse only served to fuel the wonder that surrounded the "rivalry" between him and Red Bear. Members of the tribe openly wondered if Spotted Horse's loss of prestige, his shame, and even his death were caused by Red Bear's prodigious powers.

93

Did he, in fact, use his powers against Spotted Horse, a member of his own tribe? If he did, would there be repercussions upon Red Bear himself, as the Crows always maintained? Against all of this, confidence in Red Bear, his powers, and his ability to lead did not diminish. It even appeared that his reputation was ever more on the increase.

The Years Following the Red Lodge

Top of the Mountain lived as an admired and respected member of the tribe following the revenge of Red Bear for the debacle at the Red Lodge. The Shoshones were soundly beaten and their leader, Splintered End, met his end at the revenge-minded hands of the war party.

Members would recall the many details and the heroism of the Red Bear war party, which would stand as a lasting legend of his medicine, his prodigious powers, and his unerring leadership on the warpath. The heroes of that war party continued to occupy the conversations of the tribe at the fireside, in the lodges, and wherever Crows met. There were three bands of the Crows at this time, including the Mountain Crows [main camp], the River Crows, and the Kicked in the Bellies. The stories of that revenge spread quickly among these bands and camps. Friends of the tribe quickly learned of the event, and even enemies of the Crows beyond the Shoshones knew of the crushing defeat of the Splintered End band of Shoshones and awesome prowess of the Red Bear war party and team. The names of Pretty Eagle, Old Alligator, and others became common even among enemies of the Crows.

Throughout all this, the one name that occupied the most discussion and that was repeated the most often was the outstanding hero of that fateful morning on the ice and riverbanks, Top of the Mountain. As time went by all too swiftly, it was always Top of the Mountain whose virtues and considerable abilities were put forward as literally having no equal. His reputation had become so overwhelming that even married women were said to fight over claims to be desired by Top of the Mountain.

It was to be expected, but he began to conduct himself in ways that caused people to talk about him in hushed and private tones, wondering how long it would be before the aura of heroism would become tarnished and his image of not doing anything wrong would leave him. In times of wife taking between the societies and clans, he struck fear in the minds and hearts of even his friends due to a propensity to take whichever woman took his fancy, whether friend or rival.

SHEE-SHE [HUNTS TO DIE OR LONGS TO DIE]

Top of the Mountain had acquired the name of "Hunts to Die" among the Mountain Crows following the incidents in "The Saga of Red Bear." After he began living among the River Crows, they called him *Shee-she,* meaning "Anxious" or "Longs to Die." It seemed that he was exerting every effort to live the meaning of that name: to search for hazardous and dangerous opportunities to die at the hands of the enemy. His bravery, recklessness, and foolhardiness [traits that were admired among warriors] appeared to be extended to his conduct within the tribe. People were soon saying, "He is crazy because he is Piegan," a reference to his ancestry, which included Piegan [Blackfeet] blood [Crows are quick to attribute craziness to members of that tribe].

His amorous ventures soon moved into areas that were taboo among certain members and pockets of the tribe. He would take women even from husbands and families who numbered themselves as friends and supporters. And although it was under compelling persuasions that he did so, he left the Lumpwoods and joined its keen rival society, the Foxes. This caused extreme embarrassment to the Lumpwoods, as the Foxes were given to forever reminding one and all that one of the foremost heroes of the tribe was no longer a Lumpwood, but now one of them.

In spite of the fast-developing wonder about the real loyalty and integrity of his nephew, his little brother, Red Bear continued to call upon Hunts to Die to be at his side whenever the opportunity came and to have him do those things at which he excelled on the warpath. The opportunity came often, as Red Bear himself gained even more fame and prestige. He would become a principal chief of the Crow, admired by all who would follow him and feared by the enemy and those who would gain his wrath. Much had changed since Red Bear had demolished the camp of Splintered End. White men had come to Crow Country and with them came new weapons and new opportunity. New dangers and threats came also. The coming of the white man crowded enemies of the Crows increasingly into Crow territory, raising frequent and threatening contacts between them.

Raids upon Crows by the Sioux became ever more frequent. The Crows were not always victorious in these encounters, and the thirst for revenge increased with each passing season. Hunts to Die gained ever increasing honors as battle after battle was joined with the enemy, but it seemed that his particular source of honors was fighting against the Sioux, and he was often called upon whenever the Crows rode against them.

Hunts to Die began to live more and more with the River Crows. The River Crow band was the band that roved farther east; it provided more opportunity for Hunts to Die in his continued move to gain even more honors on the warrior trail.

The Kicked in the Bellies were secure in their favorite country, beyond the mountains and the main camp, staying more and more to the upper reaches of the Elk River. Chief Red Plume on the Temple, who was known to the whites as Chief Long Hair, had signed the Friendship Treaty at Ft. Mandan, North Dakota Territory, in 1825. The Crows were to become lasting friends of the white men, never to have hostile relationships throughout the years following the treaty. These were indeed changed times.

RED BEAR MOVES AGAIN

Some Crows had recently been killed by the Sioux and revenge was again on the minds of the Crows. As the feeling for revenge became ever more bitter, the mourners filled the pipe and offered it first to one war party leader, then another. Each of the leaders seemed to find some reason not to accept until the mourners desiring revenge soon found themselves at a loss in their quest. It was then that a distant relative said, "Let us go to Red Bear."

So it was that they asked the Great One: "Red Bear, we humbly and pitifully desire revenge for the loss of loved ones at the hands of the Sioux. However, it seems that every one of the war leaders whom we have approached seems to have no desire to grant our request and wreak vengeance on the enemy and relieve our sorrow." Red Bear seemed to grow in physical stature as he responded. "All right. When times are good and things are good, they always seem to want to do those things. But why do they not accept the challenge now? Bring the pipe. I will do it."

97

With that he took the pipe and smoked regally, as he did at Iiaxupash on that fateful and memorable spring night so long ago. Those who remembered that night felt that they could sense the same gravity of acceptance now as then. When he finished smoking the pipe, Red Bear's announcement was short and to the point. "Let us proceed. Those who desire to join, do so. If the entire camp wishes to join the war party, so be it. It will be good."

The ritual of singing through the camp was impressive as a group larger than could be expected hurried to join the war party, which was now led by that great champion, Red Bear. With him as the leader, success seemed a certainty; revenge would be had. A great variety of warrior and society songs rang in the air as the party made its way out of the camp and in the direction of the hated Sioux.

The party moved deliberately and with purpose. It seemed that it had traveled much farther than reasonable, yet there was no sign of the enemy, nor was there any indication that Red Bear anticipated anything or sensed how things were going. Red Bear said that scouting was difficult on the wide-open plains. Instead he sent scouts out ahead on horseback, and these scouts swiftly covered the areas ahead of the main war party ever deeper into the land of the Sioux. But still, there was no sign of the enemy; they returned empty handed time and again.

Finally, on one of the long forays, the scouts sighted the lodges of a camp. As they came into sight of the main party, they were seen to be brandishing and waving their rifles, a clear sign that the enemy had been spotted. Quickly, huge mounds of buffalo chips were stacked, and the scouts trampled them underfoot to the sounds, "*Haa heh! haa heh!*" At the same time, there were any number of pantomimes as person after person demonstrated what he would do to the enemy.

THE THREE-MAN RAID

In a loud authoritative voice, Red Bear shouted, "Gather around and hear me. I will announce my plans here and now." Soon, the party gathered around the Great One and strained to hear his pronouncement. He said, "I am sending only three. I will pick only three to go forth to engage the enemy. Spotted Buffalo, come forth!" With that, Spotted Buffalo rode into the clearing in the midst of the gathering on his strapping dapple gray, a horse that could run all day and into the night. He was an imposing figure astride his beautiful mount for all to see as he took his place.

Red Bear continued in a loud voice: "*Shee-she!*" "All right, you too!" *Shee-she* was as handsome and athletic as ever as he took his place alongside Spotted Buffalo in the midst of the gathering. He was mounted on his beautiful, blaze-faced sorrel with stocking feet.

"Crazy Head!" Red Bear beckoned. Crazy Head, one of the all-time legendary warriors of the Crows, rode forth on the horse called the Short Gray by tribal members who knew this unusual-looking but outstanding mount.

These were the three as named by the war party chief. Only these three, Spotted Buffalo, Shee-she, and Crazy Head would go on from here. The success and failure of this war party, this quest for revenge, hung squarely on the shoulders of this distinguished and handpicked group. It was obvious that Red Bear's confidence in his versatile and distinguished nephew had not diminished in spite of recent doubts about his loyalty and integrity. Once again, *Shee-she* would venture into situations experienced by but a few. He would be placed in a situation in which he needed to be at his very best, and indeed at the very best of anyone in the tribe, given the legendary warriors that he was cast with for the success or failure of this quest against the enemy.

It was Red Bear who spoke again: "All right. This is good enough, just you three. When there are too many, they get sloppy and careless. They do not complete what is to be done. Now, you three, whether you hit him or touch him, or if you press the muzzle of your rifle against him, then pull the trigger, none of that is any good. It will not count! You have to cut the scalp. That is what will count. The one who brings the scalp to me will be the striker of the first coup. Nothing else will count. Is that clear? Is that understood?" Now the rules had been set.

"Your enemy is formidable," Red Bear said. "They are overwhelmingly large in number and they are strong. The scouts reported that there were at least four concentric circles of lodges. It is a very large camp. All right. That is it. As for me and the rest of the war party, we will return home from here. Remember what I said. Do you understand?" Red Bear asked. The three designated warriors expressed agreement.

"*Go now!*" the Great One ordered.

With that, Spotted Buffalo, *Shee-she,* and Crazy Head quickly took the trail in the direction of the hated enemy; they headed toward the Sioux camp. They were skillful and with their tried and tested warhorses, they quickly arrived at a vantage point, and there it was, a huge camp of the Sioux. As they renewed glances at the camp, it began to look even larger than that reported by the scouts. Crowded into a broad valley and extending into the plains downstream and beyond, this camp was huge.

It was broad daylight yet, so the three took cover and began what eventually would be a long vigil. They agreed that if any of the enemy ventured beyond the fringe of the camp, they would perform their designated deed then and there. So they waited, waited, and waited even more. Still no one ventured out of the huge camp that they could see. Not a single person or group ventured to check the large horse herd that was in plain sight of the three Crow warriors. Anxiety and impatience were becoming a problem with the ever darkening dusk.

One of them remarked, "This is pushing us to even more difficult situations than we anticipated. They are making it more and more difficult until our options are the most dangerous. We will need to exceed our best efforts and accomplish our mission under the most difficult of situations."

Indeed, their mission had now taken unimagined dimensions of dangers, real and imagined. The three, and only the three, were at the very edge of this huge enemy camp, full of hated Sioux who would jump at the opportunity to overcome, humiliate, and forever boast about the fate of this foolhardy collection of Crows that dared to venture into the very gun barrels of this mighty Sioux camp.

Yet, the three knew without saying it that this collection of warrior talent was so cunning and awesome that if this thrust was to be completed as ordered by Red Bear, these three were the ones who could do it. They were mounted on the kind of horseflesh that you could count on under dangerous circumstances; they knew that was what would unfold this night. Their horses were well trained, dependable, and strong and functioned as one with their respective riders. They were the best.

As night began to fall and the darkness provided cover, they said, "This is it. We have to go right into the camp and do it there [since none will come out]." As they pondered their next move, a bonfire began to blaze into prominence in the upstream part of the camp some distance from the inner circle of lodges and toward the middle of the clearing. They said, "That is the place; we will move right toward that fire and do it there."

A few moments later, another bonfire sprang up in the downstream portion of the camp. It was centrally located like the first fire but was more downstream in the midst of the lower part, within the inner row of lodges.

"That's it!" All three agreed and readied themselves.

Their mounts were readied for a quick, furious attack and a fast getaway. Their gear was tightened and their weapons made ready. With loaded guns and shortened reins, they proceeded. They moved into the camp deliberately and fearlessly, skillfully picking their way single-file and sometimes riding abreast as they passed first one row of tepees then another. In no time at all, they found themselves in the middle of the circle of lodges in the darkness, somewhere between the two bonfires. As they surveyed their position they heard someone coming from the upper bonfire toward the other fire, calling as he came. It was a young Sioux calling for his father in the darkness between the two fires. He came ever closer.

Now, the three Crow warriors could see the figure clearly as he made his way. They tightened their reins until each of the lively horses was almost rearing up, ready to lunge.

"*Now!*" they yelled.

The dapple gray sprang forward in an airborne leap as Spotted Buffalo kicked his mighty mount to the attack. Crazy Head had been in this situation many times before and would not be left behind. He leaned forward as he kicked the short gray, who was in full stride after only a short distance. The two accomplished warriors were neck and neck as they bore down on the shadow of a figure in the waning light of the fire. The Sioux man was totally unaware of the awesome charge being unleashed on him by the fearsome twosome of Spotted Buffalo and Crazy Head. *Shee-she* was literally left in the wake of the two fast-charging warriors as he kicked the sorrel to the attack somewhat behind his two companions.

"*Poom-poom!*" The muzzle blasts of the two guns sounded almost as one.

"I got him! It was I who pushed the rifle muzzle into him and pulled the trigger. I counted first coup!" It was Spotted Buffalo who shouted these words as he reined the big gray around.

"That is not so! It was I who touched him first with my gun as I fired!" Crazy Head quickly claimed the honor of first striker as he and Spotted Buffalo reined in their charging mounts.

Shee-she reined up on the now still and crumpled figure. Removing his razor-sharp knife, he quickly and skillfully hacked off a sizable portion of the scalp along with a handful of hair. This he quickly lodged in his hood and hurried on foot after his partners, who had caught *Shee-she*'s sorrel and were speedily leading him back. They were still arguing about who was the first to strike the enemy in the fearsome charge of a few moments ago.

Shee-she did not enter the furious argument but quickly mounted his horse, which the two arguing warriors had brought back to him. *"Let's get out of here!"* he said.

By now, muzzle blasts flashed in the darkness and isolated rifle reports echoed as the Sioux converged toward the area from whence the two repeated gunshots had come. Sioux voices called, "They are on horseback!" Shot after shot was aimed at men on horseback silhouetted against the two bonfires here and there. As bullets whistled past them, the three skillfully and speedily left the center of the camp and found their way back to the edge along the route they had used but a few moments before.

As they were leaving the last row of lodges, Crazy Head turned his short gray around and shouted aloud in the style of the camp announcers who made public announcements in the camps: "You pitiful prisoners and captives, look out for yourselves, try not to survive. It is I, Crazy Head. I am here now!" With that he quickly kicked his horse to catch up with the other two who had already cleared the encampment and were now heading into the darkness at breakneck speed. The pace was furious, as chaos was everywhere in the Sioux camp.

As the three disappeared into the dark, criers were rushing through the Sioux camp: "Do not follow in the darkness. We cannot see and it will be dangerous out there. Follow when there is daylight." The loud pronouncement by Crazy Head for the benefit of Crow captives in the Sioux camp was done to bolster the morale and spirits of the captives. This had been done previously when Faces Two Ways flaunted and taunted the Sioux on one of his legendary raids.

As they left the edge of the camp and regrouped for the fast getaway in the direction of where they had left the main war party, Spotted Buffalo and Crazy Head continued their argument and claim to have been the first to strike the enemy.

"It was I who struck him first. I did it first, didn't I?"

"No, it was I. I did it first."

The two competing warriors continued their disagreement. Finally, *Shee-*

she spoke as they hurried through the dark of night. "I do not know a thing about what you two did. My horse stepped in a hole and went into a somersault, so I do not know what you did." He spoke these words as he still had the key to being the first striker and the honors in his hood. He was fearful that if they should remember and learn that he was carrying the scalp that they would forcefully take it away from him. He never said anymore about it as the two continued their disputing claim. Yet, they ran and ran.

It was Crazy Head who spoke. "Crazy Head! Is it because your enemy is not to be feared and weak that you have not fled at all? You are not fleeing at all!" He spoke these words as if to deride himself as he kept an ever tightening rein on the short gray. Still, his horse covered the ground easily and seemingly without effort. Spotted Buffalo was whipping the dapple gray, and *Shee-she*'s sorrel was running so hard that, for all the world, he appeared like a small fox trying to elude a pursuer. Still, he whipped the sorrel ever more as Crazy Head reminded him, "You have not begun to flee yet, not at all!" Still, they ran and ran.

THE SUN SETS BEHIND THE HORIZON

They kept up the killing pace and ran until dawn began to bring the light of day ever closer. "Daylight is here," one of the warriors proclaimed. As day began to light up the entire countryside, it suddenly turned dark again. It was night and dark all over again. After what seemed a long time, and as they ran and ran in the darkness, light of day returned and it became day again.

Meanwhile in the Sioux camp, the leaders and others who would take up the pursuit awoke, only to find it dark again, and did not get up as they had originally intended. As they stayed in bed and some went back to sleep, the three Crow warriors maintained their furious pace as they distanced themselves from their enemy more and more with the added darkness.

Red Bear had caused the Sun to go behind the horizon, having risen once. After considerable darkness, the Sun again came out in all its brightness. Finally, the main war party was found waiting on the trail for the three raiders. As they approached Red Bear, it was Spotted Buffalo who spoke first.

"*Cheet Issaake* [Old Man Wolf—the leader or chief scout]! I was the one. I pushed the muzzle of the gun against him and pulled the trigger. I am the one, I who struck first coup!" Crazy Head quickly responded. He announced: "That is not so. It was I. I am the one who struck him. I am the one who struck coup." It was hard to hear what all was said as both Spotted Buffalo and Crazy Head renewed their disagreement for all to hear.

Shee-she broke in. "Red Bear! You said that the scalp was the first coup. Here it is. I brought it." Red Bear replied, "That is right. Bring it." Whereupon *Shee-she* took the scalp lock to Red Bear. He had not uttered a word about the scalp until they were all before the leader of the war party, Red Bear. Then he gave it to the chief.

Red Bear sang praise songs. The mission had been completed. Revenge had been wreaked on the enemy. It was *Shee-she*'s name that he recited in the praise song. He was again the first striker and the hero! Red Bear continued: "When you were leaving, I set the rules. I said that it was the scalp that was it. Whoever took the scalp was the striker of first coup. You heard me then. So it is."

And so it was that *Shee-she* owned the honor for this war party, the story of which would be told and retold as the time that "Red Bear caused the Sun to go back beyond the horizon again." This was the war party in which Red Bear once again took up the challenge to exact revenge upon the enemy and demonstrated his powerful leadership and his tremendous powers.

Upon the war party's return to the main camp, there was a great *chuule issaahilua* with lots of singing and dancing to celebrate a victorious homecoming. *Shee-she*'s standing in the tribe increased ever more. He was everything that was good. He was very good and held in high esteem.

SHEE-SHE BECOMES AN ADVERSARY

Time passed, and now it was springtime. The camp was very large and soon the call could be heard here and there, *"Huu-huuh! Huu-huuh!"* It was wife-taking time. Of all the societies and clubs, the Foxes and the Lumpwoods were the greatest of rivals. This rivalry was focused on the ability to defy death at the hands of the enemy and to attract women. The two clubs would make every effort to outdo the other when it came to these two subjects.

Shee-she was now a Fox.

Flat Belly, named after that part of the abdominal area of an animal that hangs down and appears to be a flat portion that extends from the bottom of the belly, as in a cougar, was the chief of the Lumpwoods. His lodge was a huge, huge tepee. It was in this lodge that the Lumpwoods had gathered. They heard the announcement. *"Ee-ee-eeh!"* This was shouted four times to catch everyone's attention. "Here is the little wife of Tepee Pole *[Iichiish]*. She made up her own mind. She came to *Shee-she* to be his wife."

The Foxes rejoiced. Tepee Pole had his wife taken by *Shee-she*. *Shee-she* had taken the wife of Red Bear's little brother, the younger brother of the war-party leader. The wife was very attractive, and with her taking by *Shee-she*, the victorious Foxes were splendid in their celebration, with appropriate singing and dancing. The sounds of the Fox celebration carried throughout the camp as the Lumpwoods and their friends and relatives were downcast by this latest insult and humiliation brought yet again by *Shee-she*. Still, *Shee-she* continued to take other wives of the Lumpwoods. He did this until he took four of their wives in this one camp of the Crows. He seemed to know no limit.

With the Lumpwoods in deep despair, four of the elder members said, "Let us go and look for a better way." They went outside and talked among themselves for a long time. Finally, they agreed on a course for the Lumpwoods. They loaded the pipe and brought it into the lodge of Flat Belly, where the Lumpwoods were gathered. "All right, you fellow Lumpwoods! That man out there *[Shee-she]* is putting us all down in a terrible way. Among you, there are many of you who are handsome and desired by women. Still there are others of you who are attractive and desired by women by virtue of your prowess and deeds as warriors. There is no sense in letting him out there be the only one who is man enough to do these things that he is doing. He has put us down enough! We are taking this pipe, beginning at the door. If one of you has some claim with his wife, take this pipe, accept it, and smoke it. We will return the deed. It will be our turn. We, too, will dance."

As the pipe was offered first to the one at the entrance, then continuing with the next one, no one accepted it. As they went from one Lumpwood to another, no one claimed to have any claim on *Shee-she*'s latest wife, who appeared to be even more untouchable.

As the offer of the pipe continued considerably around the circle of

Lumpwoods, the elders proclaimed in frustration: "Why are you like this? Why do you do as you are? Why do you not take this pipe? You are men! Some of you are the greatest!" Still, the refusals continued until they were now at the rear part of the lodge. There sat Flat Belly in the position of the chief. It just happened that he and *Shee-she* were camped next to each other. They were both Greasy Mouths and clan brothers.

The old men reminded their fellow members that under these circumstances, one could lay claim even if they had played man and wife or pretended to be lovers as children. They were clearly desperate as they came to Flat Belly. "Flat Belly, if you do not accept this pipe, it seems that we will not be able to do what we wanted. We will be helpless." Flat Belly spoke. "Bring it. Light it and bring it. I will give it a try." The lighted pipe was passed to Flat Belly, who smoked it regally but reverently and passed it on. Others smoked it and passed it until it was empty, whereupon it was returned to the elders, who emptied the bowl and strained to hear Flat Belly speak. He said, "I will give it a try."

Flat Belly rose, wrapped his blanket around his shoulders, and walked to where he was camped alongside his younger clan brother and close associate, *Shee-she*. *Shee-she*'s wife was sitting outside their lodge, working on some sewing that she was doing, unaware of why Flat Belly had come to her. "That guy," he said, referring to *Shee-she*, "keeps doing some things until it is probably too much. Let us, you and me, try something ourselves." Flat Belly was casual and not insistent.

The woman turned her head around, taking in her lodge and camp in a glance, and replied, "So it will be." With that she gathered up her things, put them away, and quickly joined Flat Belly back to the Lumpwood gathering.

"Ee-eeh!" was hollered four times. "*Shee-she*'s little wife has come to Flat Belly! To be his wife and be with him! All on her own free will!" As they entered into the lodge, the entire interior of the Lumpwood gathering broke into song:

> Hiilaa, baleek, hiilaa haa, Biilaa baaleek
> [Friend, I am going, friend, I come on my own].

Finally, and at long last, a Lumpwood had taken the wife of *Shee-she*. Rejoicing and derision of *Shee-she* and the Foxes filled the air. Lumpwoods who were not already on the scene hurried to Flat Belly's camp as sounds of the wife taking rang from one end of the camp to the other. Everyone knew!

In the lodge of the Lumpwoods, voices were raised for all to hear as the Lumpwoods sang a song to the unique rhythm and beat that was their trademark. The song said:

> She came on her own free will and on her own—
> and here she is!

Praise songs and loud whooping accentuated the singing and shouting as the rejoicing quickly spread throughout the camp. People came out from all over, trying to see something of what they were hearing. Older couples just stood outside their lodges and sang duets of praise songs, punctuating them with "*Haa heh, eelasxaape, haa heh*" [praising Flat Belly]!

> You are the one; you are the finest of young men,
> *haa ha hee!*

Flat Belly's lodge was shaking to the rhythm of the repeated songs of the rejoicing members. Arrangements for this were already made when Flat Belly returned with *Shee-she*'s wife. Four members secured a firm hold on each of the four base poles of the tepee. This they shook in unison with the singing so that the entire lodge shook to the singing of the Lumpwoods. Four members with the loudest voices and skilled in giving long, lingering whoops were stationed next to the singers. As the song descended into the ending part, the singer would nudge the first of these shouters. The first of the shouters would then pierce the air with a long, lingering holler. Then as this came down to an ending, he would nudge the one next to him. This continued until the air was pierced four times with the loud, high-pitched yell taken by one, then by another.

The rejoicing and continuing celebration of the Lumpwoods captivated the entire camp, as the Foxes could only cast their gaze on the ground and find things to do that would take them out of sight and away from the event. It is told that this was probably the greatest wife taking ever in the memory of the Crows. Old people sang praise songs and even non-Lumpwoods were whooping and hollering. Some say that even the dogs of the camp were yelping and barking!

"Don't take too long! Don't make it too long! Bring things right away!" The orders to give things to the new bride were quick and to the point. This was done quickly as members scurried to their camps and returned with gifts and apparel for her. In no time at all, she was dressed in an elk-tooth dress and her face was painted with spiral streaks. These streaks were the mark of women taken under these circumstances.

Mountain Chief[1] was designated as the escort for the recently taken wife of the Lumpwoods. Mountain Chief was given this honor because he was the incomparable hero of the Battle of Rainy Buttes, where he rode into the face of the enemy countless times to rescue comrades in distress and saved them by riding double back to the safety of the Crow party. By virtue of that reputation, there would be no one in the Fox lodge who could dispute his position as one to ride double on a horse and interrupt the ritual that was to ride the length and breadth of the camp, riding double and showing everyone that she was now the woman of a Lumpwood.

Mountain Chief wasted no time in decorating his horse, painting himself, and donning his war apparel. His medicine was the prairie grouse [sage hen], his paint gray clay and red ochre mixed. He fixed a bundle of wolf pelt and raven feathers on the brow of his gray horse and fastened his bow and arrow about his torso with buffalo thongs. Fully attired as for battle, he stood ready as the other members hurried to complete dressing the woman for the slow gallop through camp.

The whooping and hollering picked up again as the woman took her place behind Mountain Chief and they galloped deliberately and completely through the camp. Everyone looked on in awe. Who would dare to question Mountain Chief's right to ride double? He had done so in the face of some of the most fearful charges of the enemy upon the Crows and had ridden double to save comrades countless times. The Lumpwoods sang and danced during and after the victorious ride through the camp. Attention returned to Red Bear as the rejoicing and dancing was ending. As they fixed their gaze upon the Great One, his announcement was solemn.

"*Shee-she* will return to the Piegans. He will no longer be with us, but he will go home to them. *Shee-she* was just like anyone else of the tribe, but I took him and raised his prestige until the top of his head touched the skies; he was above everyone else and I put him there. How is it that he treats me as his enemy and adversary? He will go home to them [the

Piegans]." With that, he took his pipe stem, scored it with his knife, drove it into the ground, and repeated, "*Shee-she* will go home!"

It was shortly thereafter that more embarrassment and humiliation plagued *Shee-she*. One by one, the four wives he had taken left him and he was obliged to take back his wife [taken by Flat Belly], who returned willingly. [To take back a woman who has been taken under those circumstances is considered the ultimate in shame. The loss of prestige is immeasurable.] In the face of this sudden reversal of his fortunes and prestige, *Shee-she* left the Crows for the camp of the Piegans. Songs of derision were raised whenever the spirit moved the Lumpwoods.

Shee-she has gone home [Lumpwood melody].

When the words were repeated, they would point in the direction of the Piegans to the tune and rhythm of the song.

The loss of respect for the one-time hero was total. How could anyone such as *Shee-she* ever face the Crows again? By his own ungrateful behavior, paying no respect to others due to the stature he had attained, *Shee-she* fell from his honored position within the tribe, and people no longer had respect for him. Red Bear was even more fearsome than before.

THE PROPHECY OF THE SIOUX

The three warriors who raided the Sioux camp when Red Bear caused the Sun to return behind the horizon had killed a young boy. The lad was not yet old enough to be a warrior and was looking for his father when Spotted Buffalo, Crazy Head, and *Shee-she* mounted the fearful charge and killed him. They were confused about the rule for gaining honors, and Spotted Buffalo and Crazy Head had argued interminably about who touched him first and who had killed him. *Shee-she* had taken the boy's scalp and gained the honors for the war party. This was according to Red Bear's instructions.

It is told that the following happened among the Sioux. The parents of the slain boy went into deep mourning. They went to the hills and fasted, mourning their loss all the while. As the Sioux camp moved from one place to another, they dwelt on their grief. Before too long, the father ended his mourning and returned to camp and tried to wipe the memory from his mind. Meanwhile, the mother continued her mourning, fasting, and eternal vigil outside the camp. She could be seen in the hills overlooking the camp, but she did not return to the comfort of her home. Instead, she carried on her mourning, accepting food and comfort only as was offered by the caring ones of the camp. She followed the camp for days and days.

The Sioux camp had now moved into a very favorable camping area and things seemed to be good everywhere in the camp. The mourning woman took her usual place on one of the hills overlooking the camp when shortly a man on horseback passed nearby. She called to him and beckoned him to come to her.

She told him, "I wish you to carry a message for me. Go to that man and ask him to build four sweat lodges. Tell him to ready the sweat lodges, prepare food, and take it to his lodge. When all is ready, you come back and let me know. I will go into the sweat lodge nearest here. Men and others will go into the other three. When we come out, we will go to his lodge and we will break our fast. At that time, I will tell my story. Now, go and tell that man."

He did not waste any time but went to the designated man. He repeated his instructions about the four sweat lodges, the food, and the storytelling. The man was gracious and anxious, noting that there were many men in the camp, but she had given him the honor of doing these things. He gave thanks for the favor. The pitiful woman who had suffered grievously was now ready to end her vigil and had selected him to bring her out of mourning.

Announcements were made and before long, people came with all the necessary things, and soon four blazing fires burned near four newly constructed sweat lodges. Food was prepared and made ready as the woman had requested. The announcements included reminders that she had requested these things to be done. People came without delay as they provided willows, wood, rocks, and all the things that were needed.

Word went out that the arrangements were complete and that there would be plenty of food. They were reminded that with all the suffering she had endured, she was sure to have some good stories to tell. They invited any and everyone to come eat and to hear her story. Then, she was told that all was ready.

After they emerged from the sweat lodge and ceremony and had bathed, all who took part dressed and retired to the lodge where the food was being served. The woman told everyone there not to despair, but to eat. She told them when they had finished eating, she would tell them her story. When everyone had finished, she began.

"I am pitiful and I am poor. The Crows killed my child. All of you know that. I kept up my mourning and I was determined to keep it up until there came something that I wanted. I wanted some measure of satisfaction, some measure of revenge. In the springtime to come, just before the cottonwood leaves reach maturity, the Crows will be camped just upstream from the confluence of the Big Horn Sheep and Elk Rivers [Big Horn and Yellowstone Rivers]. There you will do battle with the Crows. No harm will come to you. There will be no casualties and there will be no wounded among you."

In a prophetic voice, she continued: "I have been given the life of the one who killed my child. I have also been given the life of the pipe carrier. I will have revenge." She finished her story by telling everyone there that wherever the camp moved, they should be at the designated place at the time she prophesied. Praise and rejoicing songs rent the air as people noisily returned to their homes. She emphasized that there would be no casualties.

Time went and soon spring was nigh. It was recalled that the woman had made a prophecy for the Sioux. Now it was time for the Sioux camp to move in position and for the meeting of destiny and prophecy.

DEATH OF LEGENDS

It is told that the leaders of the Sioux camp were always anxious to do battle with the Crows and to march against them. And so it was that the leaders methodically and deliberately moved toward the designated area [just upstream from the confluence of the Big Horn and Yellowstone Rivers, just west of present-day Custer, Montana]. As predicted by the mourning Sioux mother of the boy-victim, the sizable, combined camp of the Crows was located in the valley of the Yellowstone just upstream of the confluence of the two big rivers.

In the meantime, *Shee-she,* who had been living among the Piegans since his humiliation, had returned to be in the camp of the Crows once again. There was a trading post at that location in a place called Junction. The little community surrounding the trading post was located just north of the river and downstream from the Crow camp. This is where *Shee-she* had set up his camp, without directly joining the main Crow camp south and upstream of the river.

Unaware of *Shee-she*'s camp at that location, Flat Belly and two companions arrived at the trading post. They were looking for liquor, saying, "Let us have a few drinks and sing some songs." They entered the trading post and made it clear to the trader what they wanted. The trader, who understood some Crow anyway, told them, "I do not have any whiskey right now. I need to go get some more. You see that lodge over there? He is a Crow. I just sold him my last bottle. He has some. You might share some with him while I go to get some more for you later." The bootlegger urged them to go to the lodge that was in plain sight.

So it was that the three approached the single lodge, certain that they would now enjoy the whiskey they sought and that brought them here. Flat Belly raised the flap and, with a loud sigh, entered. Inside were *Shee-she* and his wife (the wife that Flat Belly had taken and whom *Shee-she* had retaken in shame). They were the only occupants as the three friends entered. There was surprise for all.

Shee-she was overly gracious and outgoing. "Woman, it is your husband. Prepare some food. Make it good. It is good that he has come to our lodge. Sit down, be comfortable," he said as he motioned for the three unexpected visitors to take the places of honor in the lodge at the rear of the tepee.

"*Biilapxeekaat,* it is good that you come," *Shee-she* said. He was the perfect host.

Flat Belly replied, "We came to enjoy a few drinks of whiskey."

"I have some here; sit down and enjoy, and I will go get more as there is not much here," *Shee-she* said. The quart bottle was about half-full, and *Shee-she* was quick to leave the lodge.

As soon as he left the lodge and was out of hearing, the woman hastened to tell Flat Belly: "Go. Go quickly. He means to do harm to you!" Flat Belly and his companions wasted no time in leaving the lodge and disappeared into the camp across the river. It was not long before *Shee-she* returned and asked, "Where are they? They were here when I left, and I was not gone long." She replied, "They said they were going into the little village. Did you not see them?"

Shee-she muttered, "I did not see them. I did not see them at all!"

The next day as dusk approached, *Shee-she* mounted the blaze-face sorrel and slowly rode into the Crow camp. Word quickly spread, "*Shee-she* has returned." Whereas before he was handsome to an extreme, *Shee-she* now had open sores on his neck. This he covered with a black kerchief tied around in a large bandage to hide the ugly chancres. He rode once around the periphery of the camp, returned to his lodge, and as dusk darkened and cast a weird yellowish tint to the hillsides, he mounted the blaze-face sorrel. He tipped the bottle and created a vortex in the bottom of the quart bottle as he took one final and large swallow of the whiskey. As he again entered the circle of lodges, he broke out in song:

> You thought you dared to have a husband.
> It is as if you did not have a husband at all.
> That Fox is good, that is why I choose him to be my lover.

He sang the traditional Fox song, but the words had been altered to signify a single reference. A reference to *Shee-she* when he was at the height of his glory and popularity. The sorrel was magnificent as horse and rider made their way through camp and captured the undivided attention of all who were in the camp to witness this unbelievable scene. As he exited the center of the camp, his song and words trailed off into an unashamed wailing.

> There was a time when I enjoyed everything that is good
> and I was loved and desired.
> The Crows loved me and extolled my virtues and everything was good.
> From this day forward, I will never again be privileged to enjoy that again.
> Never again!

There was not a dry eye among the witnesses as people cried with him. His shoulders were no longer square and proud, but drooped, and his head hung in shame; he was no longer the handsome and proud young legend who had occupied the minds of his people for so long. His parting words were, "I am no longer a member [worthy] of a people." The witnesses cried even more as they shared grief with *Shee-she*, whereas shortly before there was hatred and disdain for him. It was touching. He returned to his camp, unsaddled the sorrel, and turned it loose.

Now it was the next day and the morning broke clear and bright.

Suddenly, the quiet of the morning of the camp was broken by the sharp announcement of the criers: "The Cut-throats [Sioux] have already arrived at the other side of the river. Bring the horses!" The sudden flurry of activity was all over the Crow camp as warriors, young and old, hurried to ready themselves for battle with the hated Sioux. This was the beginning of the fulfillment of a prophesy.

The Crows quickly forded and swam the river to arrive on the north side, where they hastily set up a skirmish line, with both sides making repeated "bravery runs" to push the enemy back. A long ridge descending to the riverbank became the skirmish line and this was the center of the contested area. The battle was furious, with neither side gaining an advantage or giving ground.

Shortly after the standoff, Spotted Buffalo and the dapple gray rode into a fusillade of Sioux bullets and arrows. As the dust settled somewhat, the crumpled figures of the gray and his rider, Spotted Buffalo, came into clear view. They had been killed instantly and on the spot. (There would be lingering thoughts ever after that he was indeed the one who had killed the young boy in the Sioux camp.)

Still, both sides waged the battle, keeping it at an ever increasing intensity. It seemed like a long time, although time passed slowly in the ferocity of the attacks and counterattacks. Still, there was no advantage to either side.

It was *Shee-she* who appeared on the lower end of the skirmish line of the Crows. He was resplendent in his regalia, astride the blaze-face sorrel. He broke into song:

> You dared to believe that you had a husband.
> It is as if you did not have a husband at all.
> That Fox is good.
> That is why I choose him to be my lover.

It was the same Fox song he had sadly sung through the Crow camp the evening before.

> When I was a real person, when I was good and desirable,
> it was so good!
> There was always something tugging at my heart.

That will no longer be.
What I am about to do is really good.
The lingering heartache will be gone.

The other side of the ridge looked alive with Crooked Sticks, Straight
Sticks [society badges of warriors who vowed to stand their ground], and
Flat Crows [lances decorated with feathers for the full length of the staff].
It was into the midst of this mass of the enemy Sioux that *Shee-she* guided
the sorrel. He whipped his mount over and under, and as the agile, swift
horse bolted, they disappeared into the midst of the embattled Sioux. He
was never seen by Crow eyes again.

The Crows were driven steadily toward the river, with an ever increasing
intensity of bravery runs and attacks by the Sioux. Crow after Crow rode
into the face of the enemy, but still the Sioux advanced toward the river.
Crazy Head had his horse shot out from under him. The short gray's
shoulder and withers were shattered viciously, and the horse was destroyed
on the spot.

As the Sioux drove ever closer to the riverbank, the Crow forces moved
upstream. Red Bear sprang to the attack. He rode hard into the phalanx of
Sioux warriors, and as they gave some ground, two Sioux had their horses
shot out from under them, leaving them afoot. Red Bear bore down on
these two. They ran for cover behind a large drift log. As they ducked
for cover and reloaded their weapons, Red Bear pulled in front of them
and dismounted from his still-healthy horse. As he charged on foot, the
Sioux rose up and fired—not one, but several, for there were other Sioux
behind the log already when the two sought cover there. Red Bear was but
a short distance from them when the barrage was fired. It seemed that all
the shots found their mark. Red Bear was nearly cut in two at the waist and
died instantly.

Crazy Head's short gray was killed, but he himself was unharmed.
Spotted Buffalo was killed, and he was one of the two [along with Crazy
Head] who had shot down on the young boy. *Shee-she* had taken the scalp.
Red Bear was the pipe carrier, the leader of the war party. It would be told
that the Sioux woman [the mother of the young boy] had had her revenge.
The Crows mourned the loss of legends on the banks of the Elk River.

Notes

THE CROW COMMUNITY THROUGH CHANGING TIMES

1. This chapter is based on a speech given by Barney Old Coyote Jr. at the University of New Hampshire.

RABBIT CHILD: A CRAZY DOG OF THE CROWS

1. The agency referred to was located near present-day Mission Creek, Montana. After portions of the reservation were ceded to the government, including the site of the original agency, it was moved to its present location outside of Hardin, Montana.

2. Rainy Buttes is a battle of legendary proportions among the Crows. The battle took place in present-day North Dakota, beginning near present-day Bowman.

3. A fortification is called a "barrier" or "fence" by the Crows. It is hastily constructed from rocks, logs, and other materials to shield and protect the occupants. It is their territory, their haven.

THE SAGA OF RED BEAR

1. Wickiups are small, rounded huts often constructed of young tree limbs covered with branches and brush.

2. A legendary warrior and later principal chief of the Crows. He and his followers would later settle in the Big Horn Valley (Big Horn District).

3. The name refers to an underwater monster that has reached old age and senility. Early interpreters used the term "alligator" to reference unseen but feared water monsters.

4. Crows do not paint their faces in any color when in mourning. In a war-party homecoming, the face is streaked or smeared with black paint. It is not painted carefully, the black being streaked as a mark of hurried celebrating with pride and rejoicing. Putting any paint on the face of a mourner signals the end of mourning.

ELUSIVE FAME AND GLORY: THE STORY OF SPOTTED HORSE

1. The term *Outcast* describes beings that have "bald heads." They are hairless and live "without fire" in the wilds. They possess extraordinary and supernatural

powers and sometimes pass these on to mortals. The term is also used to describe men who have been overcome in battle, scalped, and left for dead. Upon recovery they are disfigured, gross, and abominable beings. It is said that the skin from the forehead would collapse and they would have to push the skin away from the eyes in order to see. They are considered evil beings to be avoided and feared, said to congregate in the Crazy Mountain region because they were not welcomed owing to their hideous appearance.

2. This name means "Where They Ran Over the Sundance Lodge," referring to a heard of buffalo that trampled a sundance lodge erected near the river.

3. The Crows refer to the river as the "Powder" or "Ash River" because the water was muddy. They noted that when fires were built along the banks, the ashes did not wash away, but stayed in the cloudy water.

THE YEARS FOLLOWING THE RED LODGE

1. Mountain Chief was the father of Old Coyote and the grandfather of Henry and Barney Old Coyote.

Glossary of Crow Terms

Alasheechiilish: Hunts to Die or Longs to Die

ash buluakussake ditchik: struck the last lodge downstream

ashe koochik ditchik: struck first coup on camp

Ashhishalahaawiio: Where the Red Lodge Was Wiped Out, also Red Lodge, Montana

Ashkish shipuo: Where They Ran Over the Sundance Lodge, Clark's Fork River

ashduucheepdaala: make like an enemy stealing into camp

Awaakeenbiash: Woman on Earth

Awachii Appuush Xishish: Badger with a Hump on the Neck

Awaxaam Aakeelash: Top of the Mountain

baachilape: a supernatural being dwelling within a person

baawittasheleetak: one without friends; no one has confidence in him

Balaxxishe: Lumpwood, as in the Lumpwood society

batchet-che: good man (chief)

Batchikaaku(h): ceremonial return of the scout or scouts

batchipe: root diggers

Biilapxeekaat: one I have shared a woman with

Bikkaashe: Shoshones, meaning "Grass Lodges"

Bilap chaashe: Powder River or Ash River

Biliiliikashee: Swift Current, or Red Lodge, Montana

Buliksaa Xaaliash: Old Alligator

Cheet Issaake: Old Man Wolf, a leader or scout chief

chuuleekissuuk: sang warrior homecoming songs happily

chuule issaahilua: a very large victory celebration

chuut daak: victory songs

daakshe ditchik: struck coup

daakshe ilaadaalia ditchik: struck coup first, struck coup without any help

Daxbitche Baa Aaxxinesh: Possessive Bear

Daxbitche Buluakssaahush: Bear Approaches Downstream

Daxbitche Hishish: Red Bear

Daxbitche Xushish: Fast Bear

Deeax Itchish: Pretty Eagle

ditch ooliok: to be struck at least four times in battle and survive

Eelasxaape: Flat Belly, referring to the flat part of the abdominal area on an animal (such as a mountain lion)

hiilla(h): term of friendship between women

huumishi: do your thing

Iaxxuke: fox, as in the Fox society or the animal

iiaxcheeteek: holding on to his tether

Iiaxupash: site of the Crow camp, Mission Creek, Montana (just south of present-day Livingston, Montana)

Iichiilixaxxish Anmaawulua: Where Spotted Horse Fought

Iichiish: Teepee Pole

Iichiilixaxxish: Spotted Horse

iilapaache: friend

ilichiin dutchik: took an enemy's horse in battle

ishadaxxia dutchik: to wrench a gun from the enemy

Kaaxu Cheete: Goes into a Frenzy Often or Frenzies Often

kootaahisht: so it is, already (emphatic way of agreeing)

Uppiluussachish: Splintered End or Split End

uuxe xape: when deer fell, period of time in winter/spring

xaxxi shiilesh dutchik: captured the sorrel paint horse

Index

Page references in italics indicate illustrations.

counting of deeds and, 15–16; war party, 56–61, 65. *See also* ceremonies; mystical powers (medicine); paint; preparation (backup)

rivalry: clans and, 5; clubs and, 17–18, 44–45, 85, 104–9; Red Bear and Spotted Horse, 57, 74, 82–84, 85–87, 93–94

River Crows: areas frequented, 76; as band, 7; Hidatsa visits by, 76; Hunts to Die and, 97; Spotted Horse as, 76, 80

root-digging tools (*batchipe*), 40–41, 42, 43, 56, 66

Runs through the Camp, 35

sage, 60

scalping, 99, 101–2, 117–18 n.1

scars. *See* sundance

scouts: ceremonial return of (*Batchikaaku*), 49, 52–54, 56, 98; clothing of, 49, 55; face paint of, 52; hair of, 50; as marathoners, 50; mystical powers of, 50; preparation for mission, 43; Top of the Mountain as, 45, 48–56; war camp chosen by, 45. *See also* war parties

Screech Owl, 33–38

sexual activity: Crazy Dogs and, 19. *See also* marriage; wife taking

Shee-she. See Top of the Mountain (*Shee-she*, Hunts to Die, Longs to Die)

"shooting down on," 16

Shoshones: as enemy of Crows, 77; physical characteristics of, 68; Red Bear's vengeance on, 40, 64–75, 95. *See also* Red Bear

Siouan linguistic classification, 3

Sioux: ceremony of Crow and, 8; Hunts to Die and, 97, 98–104; pipe offering and, 41; prophecy of, 109–15; Rabbit Child battle and, 34–38; Red Bear and, 86–87, 98–99, 103–4, 109, 115; Spotted Horse and, 80–82, 92–93

Sits in the Middle of the Land, 4, 28

smudging. *See* incense

societies. *See* clubs and societies (male)

songs: of Crazy Dogs, 20, 29–30; of Lumpwoods, wife taking, 106–7, 108, 109; of One with a Mother, 54; of Possessive Bear, 59–60; of Red Bear, 47–48; of returning war party, 69; of scouts, 53; of *Shee-she* (Top of the Mountain), 113, 114–15; of Spotted Horse, 58, 80; of war party preparations, generally, 98. *See also* calls; drums; mystical powers (medicine); trilling; war whoop

Sore Lip clan (Burned Lip clan), 6

Splintered End (*Uppiluussachish*), 65–66, 95

Spotted Buffalo, 98–104, 109, 114, 115

Spotted Horse (*Iichilixaxxish*): Arapaho war party and, 77–80; clothing of, 74, 92; death of, 92–93; horse of, 79; loss of prestige of, 88–93; mystical powers (medicine) of, 57–59, 77, 80–82, 84, 87; naming of, 76–80; and Red Lodge war party, 56–59, 74, 82–83; rivalry with Red Bear, 57, 74, 82–84, 85–87, 93–94; Sioux war parties and, 80–82, 92–93; songs of, 58, 80; youth of, 76–77

spring camp, 27–28, 40, 85, 92

spyglass use, 49, 52, 53, 55–56, 70

stories of the Crow: accomplishment of deeds as element in, 9; mysticism as element in, 9, 11; periods of, 9

storytelling: drums and, 14–15; humility and, 14–15; terminology used in, 16; truth in, 15–16; war parties and, 46. *See also* oral tradition

Straight Sticks and Crooked Sticks, 36, 115

Strikes Coup on the Ice, xxii

summer camp, 31–32, 34, 89

Sun, 46, 103–4

sundance, 15–16, 57–58, 80

sweat lodge, 110

sweet grass, 61, 65, 66

symbolic objects, uses of, 15–16